SO YOU THINK NOBODY LOVES YOU?

Robert Kelly SJ

SO YOU THINK NOBODY LOVES YOU?

VERITAS

First published 1992 by
Veritas Publications
7-8 Lower Abbey Street
Dublin 1

Copyright © Robert Kelly SJ, 1992

ISBN 1 85390 144 X

British Library Cataloguing
in Publication Data.
A catalogue record for
this book is available
from the British Library.

Cover design by Centraline Creative, Dublin
Printed in the Republic of Ireland
by Criterion Press Ltd, Dublin

Planted in love and built on love, you will with all the Saints have strength to grasp the breadth and the length, the height and the depth; until, knowing the love of Christ, which is beyond all knowledge, you are filled with the utter fullness of God.

(Ep 3:18-19)

CONTENTS

INTRODUCTION

I believe that the life of each one of us is a story, a story that has purpose, direction and deep meaning. As the story of our life unfolds there will be many things that we cannot understand at the time they happen. As we actually live out the story, we will not see the meaning of certain events and happenings. Indeed, often there will only appear to be confusion, mistakes, chance, failure, sin, loneliness. At times not only will others fail to understand us, but even we will fail to understand ourselves. Even so, I still believe that life is a story with purpose, direction, meaning. To accept this truth is a blessing and a healing experience. I hope this book may help you to understand and believe this truth about your own life, that it has great meaning and value.

I dedicate the book to the many Zambian students who shared their faith and their life-story with me in retreats over the past twenty years. Some I have met again since those days and I have listened with a sense of privilege and respect as they tell how their story is unfolding. Many others I have not met but I pray for them that they may always find the deep hidden meaning in their different stories. Quite a number have left us after completing life's pilgrimage. They now see clearly and with wonder, the richness of their own being which we, still on the way, see only darkly and, as it were, through a veil. This must be so. Our story is a faith story and there is always some darkness associated with faith. But our story is, above all, a love story. We are lovable and we are loved. If we cannot believe this, then our journey will be very hard and we shall not even want to read our own story. But if we can believe it, then, despite darkness and sorrows, there will be times when our hearts will burn within us along the way. This experience of love can be our manna as we journey to the Promised Land.

The reflections in this book are the fruit of those retreats

1

shared with many Zambian student friends. I hope they may be of some help to present-day students in finding meaning in their lives. Also I hope that former students who made those retreats and who are now learning in the school of life may be renewed in hope and courage by these pages. As an introduction to the book, let us look together at a little story.

Long ago in a certain city there lived a poor man. He was a tailor and he and his family lived in the poorest areas of that city. The street where they lived was even called Poverty Street and the family lived in the last house in that street. Because he was poor, the tailor often dreamed of riches, of the wealth that would change his life and the life of his family. One morning he woke up after a very vivid dream and excitedly called his wife to tell her his dream. He told her he had dreamt about a buried treasure. The dream was so vivid he felt it must be true. He saw in his dream a foreign city with a river running through it. There was a bridge over the river and under the bridge was a buried treasure. He trusted the dream so much, he was going to search for the city and the treasure.

So, he set out, and after passing through many strange places, he eventually came to a city which corresponded to the city in his dream, and yes, there was a river running through it. He asked local people if there was a bridge over their river and was told there was a beautiful bridge crossing the river about a mile away. The poor tailor was so eager, he ran the whole way till he reached the bridge. But now he met his first disappointment. He found something which had not appeared in the dream. Walking back and forth across the bridge was an armed soldier with a big rifle! How could he begin digging under the bridge? Surely the soldier would not understand! So, the tailor hid himself in the bushes near the bridge. Tired from his long travels he fell asleep. Soon, a passing lorry made such a noise that the poor man woke up with a start and betrayed himself to the soldier. The guard rushed over, roughly ordered him out of his hiding place and demanded an explanation. The tailor, being a simple man, told the whole truth, all about the dream and the treasure. The soldier listened with clearly growing excitement and great wonder. When the story was told, the soldier said excitedly: Listen, my poor friend, you will not believe what I have to say. I too am a poor man, for we are not well paid in this army and I too, like you, often dream of becoming rich some day. Only last night I too had a vivid dream. I dreamt of a foreign city where I had never set foot and in that city of my dream I saw a street called Poverty Street. I dreamt that in the last house of that street there lived a poor tailor and his family. In the dream I was clearly told that under the fireplace in that house a treasure was buried! I was about to ask for leave, so that I could go and look for the treasure.

This story or parable may say different things to different people. I share with you what it says to me. It is this. We do not have to make a journey away from where we are to find the treasure that can change and transform our lives. It is right where we are. The poor tailor travelled through many towns to find a treasure which was hidden in his own house. The poor soldier was preparing to journey many miles to find a treasure which was under his feet as he marched over and back across the bridge. We do not have to leave where we are and we do not have to leave who we are, to find the treasure that can make everything new. It is hidden at home. It is hidden within us. Jesus said, 'The Kingdom of God is close at hand' (Mk 1:15).

Do you remember when Jesus met the Samaritan woman at the well of Jacob? This pagan woman was very excited when she discovered that Jesus was a prophet and she immediately asked where people should go to find God. Should they go up to Jerusalem like the Jews to the Temple, or should they go up the mountain of Gerizim to the holy place like the Samaritans? Jesus answered that neither journey was necessary. God is Spirit and he is found everywhere. St Paul put it beautifully. 'The temple of God is sacred and you are that temple' (1 Co 3:17). God is within us.

In our search for the treasure that can transform our lives, a journey must be made, but not a journey of space and miles, not a journey away from where I am and not a journey away from who I am. I must make an interior journey, a journey into myself. What will I find? Let us see.

1

WHO AM I?

When John the Baptist was preaching at the Jordan, large crowds came to hear him. In Jerusalem the religious leaders were curious and worried by his popularity. They sent messengers to the Jordan to investigate. The messengers put this question to John: 'Who are you and what have you to say about yourself?' (Jn 1:22-23). I ask you to take this question into your own heart now and try to answer it. What would you say to someone who asked you: 'Who are you and what have you to say about yourself?'

You could answer by giving your name, address ad occupation. But these answers would not touch the deep self which is you, the unique person you are. Are your thoughts you, or your words or feelings or your actions, or all of these put together? No! You are the person who thinks, feels, speaks, does all these things. But who is this person, who is this self, your self? What have you to say about your self? What is the deep reality which makes you this person? What is your identity? Clearly you must journey deep within to find this person, this self. On the journey you must pass by and leave behind all the externals of your life, your age, sex, tribe, words, deeds both good and bad. You cannot be identified with any of these. You must journey deep to find what the Psalmist calls 'my inmost self' (Ps 139:13).

St Paul, in his letter to the Christians of Ephesus, makes this prayer for them: 'May God out of his infinite glory, give you the power for your hidden self to grow strong'. (Ep 3:16). Paul speaks of our 'hidden self'. He says: Our self is hidden. If I ask you 'Do you see yourself when you look in the mirror?', what would you answer? The answer should be no! In a mirror I see my face but not my self. The mirror shows me my face and how often the face is used as a mask to hide the real me!

When we make the journey within to this hidden self, what do we find? We find that the deepest core and centre of our being is good and holy and created in the image and likeness of God. We find God there at the centre accepting us and loving us. At the very moment that we arrive at this 'inmost self', no matter what the surface may be like, we find at that moment God present telling us he loves us and accepts us just as we are right now. Just as we are, not as we should be or might wish to be, but as we are. This loving acceptance of us by God present within us is the buried treasure of our dreams.

I am not alone. I am a dwelling place and the God who dwells there is not idle but is ever busy healing, recreating and renewing me. He is ever busy loving me. God never rests. In one of the Gospel stories Jesus cured a sick man on the Sabbath. Now the Jews had a very narrow idea of the Sabbath. No work, not even the work of healing, was allowed. Their idea of God was as narrow as their idea of the Sabbath. This was one reason why Jesus came, to reveal the true God. Now when Jesus cured the sick man on the Sabbath, the Scribes and the Pharisees were angry and complained bitterly to Jesus. He made an interesting reply when defending himself. He defended himself and his Father with these words, 'My Father goes on working and so do I' (Jn 5:17). There is no Sabbath from loving.

This is the God who dwells in my being every moment, breathing life into me. Indeed, we have to say that if God for one second stopped thinking of me I would cease to exist. I live each moment because God is loving me into life each moment. I am because he loves me. Eastern holy men use beautiful images to express this truth. They say the relationship between God and me is as close and intimate as the relationship between the Singer and the Song, between the Dancer and the Dance. We cannot imagine a song floating through the air without someone singing it! Nor can we think of a dance independent of a dancer. God is the Singer and I am his Song. God is the Dancer and I am his Dance. These images tell us that not only does God keep us in being each second but does so rejoicing in us. God himself uses the same image in the beautiful prophecy of Zephaniah, 'Yahweh will dance with shouts of joy for you as on a day of festival' (Zp 3:18).

Now let us be totally honest here. Perhaps you do not agree with what I have written. Perhaps you think it is not true for you. It may apply to others but not to you because right now you feel you are not good, you are not in the image of God. Just now you say you are not lovable because there is much wrong in your life, there is past evil committed, present evil desires and much weakness. So God cannot love you as you are now. If you say this, I contradict you. I say you are wrong. And I will go further and say this. Nothing you might do or say could make God love you more than he loves you right now. Put this another way. I believe that if you changed your life completely this very day and if you lived the next twenty years in prayer and fasting without the slightest moral fault, I believe God would not love you more than he does right now as you read this sentence. This is a very big thing to say. It is so big that I don't think you can say yes to this quickly and pass on. It is not easy to digest this truth. It is a very heavy saying. You cannot lightly say Amen to this and move on quickly.

This is the buried treasure of your dreams. This is the treasure buried in the field of our life which, if you find, you will sell all else to keep (Mt 13:46). This is the stream of living water which the roots of your being must reach and touch to draw nourishment that will make your life fruitful. God loves you one hundred per cent, with his whole heart at this moment as you read. Can you say Amen to this? Can you accept it? To accept God's loving acceptance of you is the secret of holiness and happiness.

Why do you hesitate? Because you know your sinfulness and want to be honest. You don't want to pretend or be a hypocrite. That is good. We could never build holiness or happiness on pretence or hypocrisy. But just now I ask a favour. For the moment I ask you to forget about your sins, about all the mean, ugly part of yourself which troubles you. I promise we will return to this later and face it honestly, but just now listen to God telling you that he knows you now as you are, he knows every twist and turn of your heart, every secret corner of your soul, knows your depths even more clearly than you do and still says: 'I accept you and love you'.

Ask for the gift of the Holy Spirit to help you say Amen to this. The Spirit of God helps us in our weakness. God's spirit will help you to accept the unique and wonderful gift of your own innermost self which God sees and loves at this moment. When you do accept then you will be able, sincerely and joyfully, to thank God for the gift of your own self. This is a wonderful prayer. In no way is it pride to rejoice in your own true self. It is great humility and true worship. It is humility, for you are confessing that you are not your own creator, you are from God, you are God's gift. And it is worship, for you are giving God the praise and the glory. It is the prayer of the Psalmist:

> It was you who created my inmost self
> and put me together in my mother's womb;
> for all these mysteries I thank you;
> for the wonder of myself,
> for the wonder of your works. (Ps 139:13-14)

This is the kind of love of self Jesus spoke of when he said: 'You should love your neighbour as yourself' (Mt 22:39). Let us stop wishing we were someone else. Let us stop rejecting the gift of self God has given us. God wants to introduce us to our true self in which he rejoices. Let us too rejoice and praise him. Let us celebrate our birthday each year with a new sense of joy and wonder. I am sure God celebrates it. Each one of us is a unique creation. There is no other person in the universe like you and never will be. God does not make duplicates and certainly he does not make rubbish. God created me as I am. He knew what he was doing. He wanted me.

I was once asked during a retreat 'Does God love us all equally?' I was not sure what to answer. I felt the person who asked thought that God favoured some people more than others. I believe God has no favourites in the way we think of this. So, I answered as best I could and said, 'Yes, God loves us all equally'. That was years ago. Today I would answer the question differently. I would not use the word 'equally'. I think the word does not bring out clearly the deep truth about God's love. It seems to suggest that God's love is some kind of substance that can be cut up into equal shares between us all. This gives a very poor idea of God and his love. Today I prefer to say: 'God loves each one of us uniquely.' That is, God loves me in a way he can love no one else, because there is only one me and he puts all of himself in that special love for me. God is in love with me and in that love affair he will be faithful forever. It is an everlasting love. God will never withdraw his love, he will never tire of me, never grow bored with me. I may get tired of him. I may go away from him. If so, he will wait in hope and with desire. If I turn round, he is there with open arms. This looks like foolish love. They say lovers are foolish, don't they! But only God could love like that. He loves like that because he is God, he is Love. He loves me that way not because I have earned it or deserved it, but because he is God. We say God's love is unconditional. There are no strings attached. It is not given as a reward for fulfilling some condition. It is given because that is God's very nature. God can only love. But perhaps we should qualify that statement that God's love is unconditional. There is one condition I must fulfil before I can enjoy this gift. The one condition is that I must accept his love.

2

UNCONDITIONAL LOVE

How can we understand unconditional love? We are not used to it. So much of our human love is given only on certain conditions: 'You must do what I say. You must measure up to my standards. You must give me what I want. You must please me.' Such love, of course, is not love at all, because I am at the centre, not the other person. That kind of love is some kind of reward offered to another person for pleasing me. True love is never a reward or a bribe and is never selfish.

Consider a simple human situation. As a priest I often have the joyful experience of being invited to celebrate and share the joy of a family when a new baby is born. It may be at the baptism in the church or at the celebration in the home. On such occasions we can all clearly see the great love and pride of the parents for their newborn baby. Every glance, word, gesture tells us of the warm accepting love that surrounds this precious child. Imagine if I was foolish enough to ask the mother why she loved the baby, if I said to her, 'Why do you give so much love to this baby, this baby who can do nothing for you? Your baby is too small and weak to help you in any way and only gives you extra work and keeps you awake at night! Why do you love the baby so much?' The question is so foolish we cannot imagine anyone asking it. But if the question were asked, what would the mother reply? She could only say something very simple but very deep like: 'I love her because she is mine.'

In the prophet Isaiah, God tells of his love for his people, of his love for you and me in these words:

> Do not be afraid, for I have redeemed you.
> I have called you by your name, you are mine.
> You are precious in my eyes and I love you. (Is 43:1,4)

And further on in the same prophet God says that even if the young mother we have been speaking about should forget her baby, he, our God, will never forget us.

> Does a woman forget her baby at the breast
> or fail to cherish the son of her womb?
> Yet even if these forget
> I will never forget you. (Is 49:15)

The mother loves her baby because it is her baby. If we ask the mother what the baby does for her, she can reply: 'My baby exists — it is enough.' God loves me because I am his, not because I do things for him or because I keep his laws. I don't have to earn God's love. It is a gift. A gift is not a reward. A gift is given to you because you are loved, not as payment for work done. That is why a gift is so precious, even if it has no great money value.

God gives us many gifts but the first and greatest is the gift of my own self made in his image and likeness. I come from God, from his heart. These days people have become very interested in tracing their origins, studying their family history, searching for their roots. Many are fascinated by origins and beginnings and want to know all about their family history, to go back as far as possible in their family story. And this searching for roots is not a mere intellectual exercise, it is not pursued out of mere curiosity. No! This is something deep in human nature. There is some kind of healing effect, a kind of health-giving force in tracing my origins, my story, in establishing my identity. It creates a sense of belonging. I am not isolated. I belong. It gives meaning.

We are all interested in our origins. Where do we come from? Has anyone then got the answer to that big question? Where am I ultimately from? Only one person can answer this question: our Heavenly Father. He tells us, through the prophet Jeremiah:

> Before I formed you in the womb I knew you
> before you came to birth I consecrated you. (Jr 1:5)

And again we listen to the Psalmist:

> It was you who created my inmost self and put me
> together in my mother's womb. (Ps 139:13)

Can I believe this about myself? I exist because God had me in his heart and mind and wanted me born. And since we believe God is outside time, we must go further and say that in some mysterious and wonderful way I was in God's heart from all eternity. It is this me that God loves. This is my hidden self. As I have said, we will not see this self when we look in a mirror. If we want to see this true self, we must look into God's eyes. His eyes of love will reflect my true self.

Perhaps you are still troubled by that other self which you know only too well, the ugly, mean and sinful side of you. We will come to that soon, but for now, here is a thought which may help in the meantime. When we say God accepts us and loves us as we are right now in all our sin and weakness, we are not saying that God wants us to remain that way. Look again at St Paul's prayer for his Ephesian friends:

> May God out of his infinite glory give you the power through his Spirit for your hidden self to grow strong, so that Christ may live in your hearts through faith, and then, planted in love and built on love, you will with all the saints have strength to grasp the breadth and the length, the height and the depth, until knowing the love of Christ which is beyond all knowledge, you are filled with the utter fullness of God. (Ep 3:16-19)

Notice that Paul prays for our hidden self to grow. And

then reminds us of the real secret of true growth which is love. We will grow if we are 'planted in love'.

Go back for a moment to that young mother and her newborn baby. This baby is weak and helpless. It cannot form words or reason in any way. It can only receive. Yet the mother gives it all her love. She accepts the baby totally as it is now. This does not mean that she wants the baby to remain weak and helpless. She wants her baby to grow and become a beautiful and wonderful person. So it is with God and us. He accepts us now in all our weakness and brokenness, but he does not want us to remain in that state. He wants us to grow and become the wonderful people he knows we can become. And in his wisdom he knows the secret of that growth is love. The young mother got that wisdom from God. She gives all her love to her baby as it is now, because only in such a climate of warm accepting love will this baby grow in a truly human way. Paul has this wisdom. He knows we cannot grow unless we are loved. He prays that we be planted in love. When you see a beautiful flower or shrub in bloom you know that it must have had its roots firmly planted in nourishing soil. If we are to grow properly, our roots must be planted in the nourishing soil of God's love.

Surely it is true that love releases hidden springs of growth. When we experience love are we not transformed? When we find that someone loves us just for what we are, do we not begin to feel new and better? One definition of a friend is: 'One who knows all about you and still loves you'. When we are with such a friend, we can relax, we can be ourselves, we don't have to pretend or wear masks, and we can grow. Love brings out the best in us. We can understand the words once spoken by a young man to his beloved. He said, 'I love you, not only for what you are, but for what I am when I am with you.'

A most important characteristic of true love is that it always makes the other person feel good. It never makes the other feel mean, bad or inferior. It makes the other feel good, worthwhile and lovable. It touches the deep hidden self and opens people's eyes to their own worth and beauty.

The guiding inspiration in the life of Mother Teresa of Calcutta is her awareness of people's need for love. She offers that love especially to the rejected in society. When she finds some rejected person on the point of death she gives that person all her loving care during the last moments of life even though the person will not recover. It is told that as she cradled one old dying man in her arms, the man, who was disfigured by disease and dirt, looked up at her and said: 'How strange that I, who have lived like an animal, should die like an angel.' This is the effect genuine love can have. Love that is given not as a reward for some achievement, not as a bribe to get something done but just as a gift, given to someone who is lovable in themselves. This is God's kind of loving.

3

THE OTHER HIDDEN SELF

The Good News brought by Jesus was that God loves us because we are, not because we are good. If we can believe in this unconditional love, God's kind of loving, then we can be transformed, we can be liberated and can begin to grow. But many of us have great difficulty in accepting this truth. We find it hard to believe that God loves us in that totally accepting unconditional way. Why? Let us try to answer this question now. Each of us will have his or her own answer but I believe most of us would give substantially the same answer and it would be something like this:

> God could not love me in the way you describe, because I have failed him so often in the past. I am in no way worthy of this love. This God is all holy and I am very far away from him and holiness. You speak of my hidden self and say it is good. But you are wrong. It is true I have a hidden self but it is bad and that is why I hide it and want to keep it hidden. I am always pretending, wearing masks because I want people to respect, admire and love me. I am full of meanness, selfishness, evil desires, pride. I envy the success of others and even rejoice in their failure. I find it impossible to forgive. My heart is full of lust, anger, fear. You tell me to love myself. But when I look inside and make the interior journey you speak of I want to hate myself. I don't even want to make the interior journey because I'm afraid of what I will find. Yes, I have a hidden self and wish to keep it hidden, because I am ashamed of it.

Very many of us, myself included, have thoughts like this. It is good that we should let these thoughts be exposed and that we should face up to the full picture. One thing is sure, we will never discover the truth, we will never experience the healing power of God's love if we pretend. We must hide nothing before God. We would fail completely in our search for love and happiness and meaning, if we pretended all was well, if, when we spoke of our hidden self, we closed our eyes to the bad and evil within us. The wonderful joy and peace that can come to us when we are told that God loves us as we are, would be counterfeit if we did not at the same time admit and confess our evil side. Indeed all the real value of our early reflection in this book would be lost because it would be a kind of cheating. If we are going to find the truth which can be the only safe foundation for our life, then there must be no hiding or pretending. The foundation of our lives must be rock, not sand.

So, let us humbly and honestly admit there is an evil side, a weakness and selfishness that leads us often to betray God and our own best self. Does that mean that what we have said is less true, that my hidden self after all is not good, that God does not love me as I am? In no way. Indeed it is here, now, that we enter into the deeper understanding of what true love is like, God's kind of loving. Indeed I would say that we shall never properly appreciate the full wonder of God's love until we honestly face the fact that we are sinful people. It is true that we are sinful people, but to this we must immediately add, a sinful people who are redeemed, a sinful people who have been forgiven. These two truths must always be held together. When they are held together, and believed together by the heart, then we are on the road to true love, joy and peace. G.K. Chesterton, the famous writer and convert to Catholicism, gives this definition of a saint. He says: 'A saint is a sinner who knows he is forgiven.' Yes, I am a sinner, but I am forgiven. There are two truths here which, as I say, must be believed together. If I stress one at the expense of the other I am in trouble. If I stress my sinfulness without the conviction of being forgiven I am heading for despair and will lose joy. Or if I lightly say I am forgiven without believing I am a sinner then I miss the true salvation Jesus brought. It is when I stand honestly before God and thank him for the gift of self and go on to admit my weakness and failure and how I mess up his gift in myself and others, it is precisely then that I experience the incredible love of God, that I experience God smiling at me, taking me in his arms, telling me he understands and forgives. Yes, God sees the badness in you but still loves you. He knows this hidden self of which you are ashamed. But he knows more. He knows this is not your real true self. He is able to see deeper still into your being, to the goodness that is at the centre. Loving eyes will always see past faults and failures to the deeper good. God trusts us more than we trust ourselves. God wants to introduce us to our deepest, truest self. This is love and it makes it possible for us to grow out of evil and sin.

How can we be so sure of all this? Because we have been told so by God in Jesus. In the letter to the Hebrews we read that God at various times in the past spoke to his people through the Prophets. God's message was always one of love, inviting us to love him and each other. But people were so discouraged and oppressed by sin, that God finally sent his Son to liberate them and give them new life and new power to become what he wanted them to be. The message was so important and God was so serious, that he would not rely any more on spoken words, or on prophets. He would at last speak through his Son. And so, God's word became flesh. God became visible in Jesus. God's love could now be seen and touched in Jesus. At long last people could know what God thinks of us in our sinful state.

Later, we shall look carefully at Jesus and see how he tried so hard by word and deed to reveal God's compassion for the sinner, to convince us that God knows us in all our weakness and sinfulness and still loves us. St Paul says that is the great proof of his love, that he died for us while we were still sinners, even before we had changed (Rm 5:8). This truth about God's total acceptance of us as we are is so important for our Christian life that we can expect Satan our enemy to tempt us to doubt it. Satan fears more than anything else the power of God's love. Satan wants us to live in fear of God. Fear came into the world through sin. When our first parents sinned we are told they hid themselves because they were afraid (Gn 3:10). When Christ came to reverse that sin and all its effects he constantly greeted people with the words, 'Fear not'. St Paul insists that we have received Christ's Spirit, which is not a spirit of fear, but the Spirit which makes us cry out 'Abba!' (Rm 8:14-17). We are children of God. When we accept this in a childlike way we can begin to grow as members of God's family. Satan does not want this. So, he tries to sow doubt in our hearts. He reminds us of our sins and failures. He wants us to despise and hate ourselves. He is the father of lies and so when God tells us of his great love Satan contradicts his word. When God reveals to us our true identity as his children, Satan tries to make us doubt his word.

Do you remember the story of the baptism of Jesus in the Jordan? When Jesus was baptised, the voice of God was heard saying: 'You are my beloved Son, my favour rests on you' (Mk 1:11). Immediately after this Jesus went into the desert to pray and, we are told, he was tempted by Satan. How did Satan tempt him? He tried to make Jesus doubt his Father's word. He began the temptation by saying, 'If you are the Son of God, tell these stones to turn into loaves' (Mt 4:3). Notice these words, 'If you are the Son of God'. Just before this, Jesus had heard his Father's word: 'You are my beloved Son'. Now Satan tries to sow doubt: 'If you are the Son. Maybe you are not. Maybe it was not God's voice at the river. Maybe it was only thunder. Maybe you imagined it.'

We are also given the revelation by the Spirit that we are sons and daughters. We can expect the same temptation. Satan will remind us of our sins and try to persuade us that God just could not love us the way we have been saying. We must not listen to the Father of lies. We must answer him as Jesus did in the desert: 'Man lives on every word that comes from the mouth of God' (Mt 4:4). Jesus himself knows how we get discouraged by our sins and feel we cannot be God's children. He told a story once of a young man, a young son who left his father's home and went abroad and wasted the family money in an evil life and disgraced the family name. When this young man eventually began to reflect on what he had done and how bad he had been, he was also tempted to think he could not be a son anymore. He decided to go back to his father and say: 'Father I have sinned against heaven and against you; I no longer deserve to be called your son; treat me as one of your paid servants' (Lk 15:18-19). What did the father do? He dressed his boy in the best robe and gave him a ring of honour. He prepared a feast and organised a celebration. These things are not done for a servant. 'The Spirit you received is not the Spirit of slaves bringing fear into your lives again; it is the Spirit of sons and it makes us cry out, Abba, Father' (Rm 8:14-15).

If we want to know our true identity, let us listen to God's Spirit. Let us not listen to the lies of Satan. Also, let us not listen to the voice of the world around us, which rejects God's Spirit. This world cannot tell us who we are. This world has its own standards of importance and value and worth. We know these standards. You must succeed, have power, money, influence before the world considers you to be somebody. If you measure up to these standards, you are important and admired. You become a VIP. You may have a police escort when you drive through town and can go through the VIP door at the airport! We may smile at this, but we have to be careful not to allow these standards, constantly put before us by the media and advertising, to become the yardstick of our own value, dignity and worth. It is the revealed word of God that gives meaning to our lives. It is Jesus who tells us who we really are and gives deep and wonderful meaning to our lives. Thanks to the gift of faith we believe in God's revelation, especially as found in Jesus.

Before we go on to look more closely at God's revelation in Jesus, let us consider the gift of faith.

4

I SEE BETTER WITH MY HEART

Have you ever watched your baby brother or sister sitting on the floor turning over the pages of a magazine or picture-book? Since they are not yet able to read, we wonder what the pictures mean to them. They can probably identify some objects in them, but because they cannot read the words which explain and interpret the pictures, they lose much of the meaning. In a way, life is a great picture-book. Every day we turn the pages and new scenes, new events unfold before our eyes. But many of us are like those children. We see what is happening but fail to find any deep meaning. We cannot read life's story. Indeed for many it is not a story at all. It is a succession of events, many of them apparently chance or accidental. There seems to be no unity, no unfolding story, no meaning.

If we see life as a story and discover meaning in it, then we have to look at life with eyes of faith. Faith enables us to look beneath the surface happenings of each day to the deeper reality underneath. Faith is a kind of language which helps us interpret the picture of life. It is a new way of seeing. One of my favourite posters shows a large shaggy dog with lots of hair hanging down over his eyes. The caption reads: 'I see better with my heart'. There is deep truth here. We see in some ways with the heart. We do not see the whole of reality with the eyes of the body. For many people, unfortunately, the only things that are real are those that are seen with the eyes, which can be known by the senses, which can be measured by scientific instruments. In our modern world, science has made fantastic progress. We are awed by its discoveries. Science deals with what can be seen, touched, measured. But many people are so intimidated by science that they believe faith is old-fashioned, a form of superstition to be discarded. But this is panic and even contradicts our own experience of life. Is it true that the only reality, the only real things are those that can be seen, touched and measured? Is it not the very opposite that is true, that the most real things in life are those that cannot be seen with the eye or the microscope?

> In a certain hospital there was a well known surgeon who was an atheist. He did not believe in God. Working with him was a nurse who was a strong believer. They often had friendly arguments about God and religion. One day they worked together for many hours in the theatre on a difficult operation. When they were relaxing after the operation, the surgeon said to the nurse with a smile, 'Sister, I was just thinking that all the time we were in the theatre and had the patient opened up and were exploring his body, I never saw any sign of that soul you are always speaking about!' The sister smiled as she answered and said: 'Doctor, isn't it also curious that in all that time I never saw any sign of the pain you were trying to take from the patient!'

We cannot see pain. Does that make it less real?

When I preside at weddings, there are always plenty of photographers getting the snaps that will later appear in the wedding album. I often say to them, 'No matter how powerful your equipment, it cannot photograph the most important reality here today, namely, the love of the young couple'. You can snap them exchanging rings, signing the book, cutting the cake, but you cannot snap their love which has made all the rest possible and gives all the meaning to their lives. Later at the reception, lots of photos are taken of the celebrations. The photographers can snap the people laughing, dancing, celebrating, but they cannot photograph the joy which is the source of all the celebration. Sometimes at funerals photos are taken of the grave and the mourners, but no camera can photograph sorrow. Yet, are not love, joy and sorrow the great realities of life?

The truly real things are hidden under the externals of life. The deeper meaning hides beneath the surface of daily events and happenings. In one of our songs we ask, 'Have you searched for the great hidden meaning?' The meaning of life is hidden but very real. Just as we said about our own true identity, what Paul called our 'hidden self', it is not seen on the surface, it is not seen in the mirror.

Many of us have been present at a flag-raising ceremony. We stand with respect as the flag of our country is raised and we sing the national anthem. If we look at such an event only with our eyes and don't look for any other hidden meaning, surely it must appear to be very odd behaviour. A crowd of intelligent people paying respect to a piece of coloured cloth! But we know that a national flag is more than a piece of coloured cloth. It is a sign, a symbol of our land and people, of the struggle for freedom and independence. People are ready to fight and die under this flag for the values it stands for.

In a marriage ceremony one of the highlights is the exchange of rings. The ring in itself is a small object and in many cases may not be very expensive but it has deep meaning for the couple. It is a symbol of unbroken love and fidelity. Later on, if either partner was to give back the ring, this gesture would reveal a terrible, painful reality — that their love was dead.

Yes, the truly real things in life are those we do not see with the eyes. Faith sees these. 'Only faith can prove the existence of the realities that at present remain unseen' (Hb 11:1). What we see with our eyes are signs pointing to the deeper reality. The photo, the flag, the ring and the dancing help to put us in touch with the deeper things that really matter and give life meaning. We must learn to read the signs, otherwise we will always remain on the surface of life. In the East there is a saying: 'When the wise man points to the moon, the fool only sees his finger.' The wise man points to the beautiful moon inviting us to look at it and admire its beauty; the fool, the man without wisdom, only sees his finger. He looks at the sign, the pointing finger and misses the beautiful reality to which the finger points. On our travels, especially in unfamiliar places, we depend much on signs to point the way and guide us to our destination. How foolish we would be if we were to stop at a signpost and go no further!

Our lives are full of signs pointing to a reality more wonderful than ourselves. There are the wonders of nature which invite us to look beyond themselves to a creator. The daily events of life are signs. Some are joyful, like a family meal, a celebration of birth or marriage, unexpected news from an old friend, a surprise gift, a cheerful greeting, a kind deed. Some may be sorrowful like a sickness, a failure in exams or work, being let down by a friend, an argument, a bereavement. Many may appear trivial in themselves. But God is somehow present in all these and speaks through them as he does through the living words of scripture. It is here in this everyday stuff of life that we must look for God, for that is where he is, in sorrow and joy, telling us there is more here than meets the eye, there is something here greater than ourselves. In sorrow he is telling us he is present, is concerned and offers power to hang in and struggle on, and promising that the sorrow will be turned into joy. In joyful events he is telling us he celebrates with us and that it is for this we are made and that it shall be our final state. In all the sorrowful and joyful mysteries of our life he is present and active. Remember the answer Jesus gave to those who complained when he cured a sick man on the Sabbath day: 'My Father goes on working and so do I' (Jn 5:17). God never rests from loving. This is what Jesus meant when he said: 'The Kingdom of God is close at hand' (Mk 1:15).The Kingdom of God is not something that is, it is something that happens.

It is God celebrating with us in the joyful events and God suffering with us in the sorrowful events.

All this is revelation. Do not think of revelation as just something from the past — things which Jesus did and said in the past which have been handed to us to study as we might study ancient history or some ancient language. Revelation is happening now through the great variety of daily events in our lives and through the living word of scripture. Revelation is a 'today' thing, a 'now' event. Someone said it very well: 'Revelation is a matter of now or never.'

If revelation is not happening for me right now, then it is never happening. It must be so because God is love and God is activity. Do I wish to get in touch with the deep hidden meaning? Am I searching for God in the world?

Here is a story about a little Jewish boy called Levi.

> He went out into the woods with his young friends to play a game of hide-and-seek. Near the end of the day it was Levi's turn to hide. He chose a good hiding place and waited to see if his pals would be able to find him. But, sad to say, by now his young companions were tired and hungry and did not trouble to search. They ran off home! Poor little Levi noticed the silence and came out of his hiding place. He was terribly upset and ran home, crying the whole way. His father who was a rabbi was standing at the door. Levi threw himself into the big strong arms of his dad who cradled him against his chest and asked why the tears. The little boy explained tearfully: 'I was hiding and no one was looking for me.' The rabbi dried his son's tears and, with a tear in his own eye, said: 'And so, my son, it is with God, he is hiding in our world and few are looking for him.'

God's greatest revelation of himself was in Jesus. Paul says 'Jesus is the love of God made visible' (Rm 8:39). And

Jesus himself said 'He who sees me sees the Father' (Jn 14:9). At the same time, paradoxically, we have to say that God's greatest hiding place was in Jesus. Faith vision was needed to see God in Jesus. Many people met Jesus, saw what he did, yet failed to believe in him. Indeed they rejected him. Why? Because he did not suit their idea of God. How dangerous to have your mind made up before-hand about what God is like! In the following pages we are going to look at Jesus and search for God in him. Let us be careful. Our familiarity with the gospel story could be dangerous. We are familiar with Jesus, his teaching and miracles. Maybe we have our minds made up and so could lose the impact of the revelation that is going on now. Let us approach with open mind and heart, ready to let the Spirit guide us to Jesus and to let Jesus bring us to the Father: 'No one can come to the Father except through me' (Jn 14:6). The only true God is the God revealed in and by Jesus.

5

FRIEND OF SINNERS

God has revealed himself to the world in Jesus of Nazareth and yet God is hidden in Jesus. We must look at Jesus with faith to find God and we must look with humility, allowing him to teach us and not imagining that we already know what God is really like. Let us spend some time looking at Jesus and learning about God. We approach with a great sense of wonder, for we are entering the infinite mystery of God and also with a sense of joy that we who are so small are being invited to look upon the glory of God. Jesus himself said, 'Many prophets and kings desired to see what you see and never saw it, and to hear what you hear and never heard it' (Lk 10:24). Above all we must come with a great sense of openness and readiness to learn. We cannot have preconceived ideas of God before Jesus reveals him.

We noticed already that those who rejected Jesus and rejected God in Jesus were not sinners but the leaders and teachers who felt sure they knew God and his ways. What did Jesus say about them? One day Jesus was warning his apostles of the opposition, and even persecution, they could expect from these men, and then he said: 'They will do these things because they have never known either the Father or myself' (Jn 16:3). Let us not make this mistake. We have many ideas about God. We feel we know how God thinks, loves, forgives, acts. But some of my ideas may be wrong, some may have to change and all my ideas will have to grow and be purified as life goes on. God is God. God is infinite Mystery. I cannot enclose him in a word or definition. He is always greater than I think. It is inevitable that many of our ideas about God are borrowed from our knowledge of ourselves and each other. We can easily slip into the idea that God thinks, acts, loves, forgives in the same way as we do, but perhaps to a greater degree. This is not so and cannot be so. God's ways and thoughts are as far above ours as the heavens are above the earth (Is 59:9). To admit that we cannot know God in the way we thought we could should not cause us anxiety but should, rather, fill us with wonder and joy and praise. Our whole life is an exploration of the wonder and mystery of God.

Earlier in this book, when we reflected on God's total, loving, unconditional acceptance of us just as we are now, we felt uncomfortable and objected that God could not accept us because we are sinners. How can I be so sure of that? Do I know how God loves? Unfortunately I think I do because I transfer what I know of human love to God and believe he must be like that. I argue this way: 'God is all holy. I am a sinner. I am not holy. Therefore God is angry with me and cannot love me until I change.' Is all this true? How can I know? Do you think God is angry with you when you sin? I don't think so. You see, we are all presuming we know what God's holiness is like. But how could we know this? Does this mean we cannot know God? No! Certainly we can never fully know God, but we can search for him in Jesus and we can learn when Jesus is our guide and the Holy Spirit our teacher. 'No one knows the Father except the Son and those to whom the Son chooses to reveal him' (Lk 10:22). Let us look at Jesus and see what he reveals and teaches.

We read in the gospel that one of the names given to Jesus was 'friend of sinners' (Mt 11:19). Does this surprise us? Think of it — the all-holy God says he is coming to be one of us and to live among us. What company would you expect him to keep? If we are honest we should say, 'He will be a man apart. He will probably be found in the company of religious teachers. He might live in some holy place, a temple, a sacred mountain, and occasionally give audiences to select people. He will take care to avoid common sinners lest he be contaminated.' But when we pick up the gospels, what do we find? Jesus is constantly in the company of those who were branded public sinners, corrupt tax collectors, drunkards, women of bad reputation, those who broke the sabbath. And he was in their company not to denounce and terrify them, but to offer his friendship. He eats and drinks with them, so that he is even accused of being 'a drunkard and a glutton' (Lk 7:34). When John the Baptist came, he waited at the Jordan for sinners to come to him, but Jesus seeks out these strange friends and for this life-style he is dubbed 'friend of sinners'.

Here is a strange situation. God is judged by people! Many people think of God as the judge, a stern judge trying weak people. But in fact it is the other way round. God is the one who is on trial. God is being judged by people and the charge is: 'He is a friend of sinners. He is giving religion a bad name!' How does God defend himself? How does Jesus answer his accusers? He answers with a brief parable. We know it so well but let us be careful not to miss its deep revelation of God's inner heart. Jesus says: 'It is the sick who need a doctor' (Lk 5:31). To defend himself Jesus looks for an image to explain how he sees sin and the sinner, how God sees sin. He takes the image from medicine and sickness and healing. He compares God to a healer and the sinner to a sick person. Notice he does not pick the image of a judge. Indeed, he rejected that image: 'I have not come to condemn but to save' (Jn 12:47). He sees himself as a doctor wishing to heal, to restore health and allow growth to continue. And he sees the sinner as one who is suffering. The evil in us leads us to act in a way that injures our own self and others as well. The only real interest Jesus has in our sins is that they bring suffering to those whom he loves so much. He has come to heal, not only the wounds caused by individual evil acts, but much more, the very root of the evil in us. Only Jesus can do that and his medicine is his unconditional love, love that is offered because it is love. A priest once shared with me this insight he had received in prayer: 'I became convinced that God loved me most where I liked myself least.' St John says, 'We are to love, then, because he loved us first' (Jn 4:19). God first loved us. First, before we had turned to love him. Jesus who is God is the friend of sinners.

Let us look at one of his sinner friends. One of Jesus' first disciples and one of his best friends was Peter the fisherman. From what we know of Peter and what we think we know of God, they seem to be an unlikely pair to become friends. How did it happen? One morning Jesus takes a walk by the lake shore. Peter is there cleaning his nets. He and his friends are weary and disappointed. They have fished all night and caught nothing. They are looking forward to breakfast. Now Jesus comes along and greets them. He asks if he may sit in Peter's boat while he teaches the crowd who were following him. Peter agrees and then, when Jesus had finished teaching, he suggests that Peter and his friends should let down their nets again and try for a catch. The men look at Peter, and Peter looks at Jesus. This Jesus is a carpenter and can know little about fishing. Peter, the experienced fisherman, knows the morning is a bad time for fishing. But something about Jesus touches Peter and he agrees. 'Master, we have worked all through the night and caught nothing, but at your word we will put out the nets' (Lk 5:5). The fishermen put out the nets and then swing the boat around in a big circle. As they begin to haul in the nets slowly and evenly they know they have caught something. The ropes are jumping in their hands and the nets are heavy to pull. The excited fishermen know they have a very large catch, so large they even have to call another boat. Jesus shares their joy and is looking intently at Peter.

Now, something very interesting happens. Peter acts in an unusual and unexpected way. We could have expected him to shout out happily, to thank Jesus, to start giving orders, to begin calculating the value of the catch. This we would expect from a fisherman. But Peter does none of these things. He is thinking deeply, he is reading the signs, he is finding a deeper reality. This Jesus must be someone very special, indeed very holy, close to God. As Peter realises this, he thinks to himself of his own lack of holiness, his sins, that hidden self which he wanted to keep hidden from others. Peter feels completely unworthy to be in the boat with Jesus. He feels a hypocrite being given this great catch of fish when he is such a bad man. If this Jesus had only known what Peter was really like, he would not have picked his boat. He might have picked John's boat. He would not have picked him and given him this catch of fish. Poor Peter is overcome and as he so often does in the gospels, he shouts out in his impulsive way what is happening in his heart: 'Depart from me Lord, for I am a sinful man' (Lk 5:8). We are lucky Peter is so honest, for now we shall learn more about God. What will Jesus say to Peter's confession? Will he leave Peter when he hears he is a sinner? We look at Jesus and wait for his answer. Jesus looks steadily into Peter's face. Perhaps he is smiling. No, Peter, I will not depart from you. I want you to be my friend and companion and I have a great work for you to do. 'Do not be afraid; from now on it is men you will catch' (Lk 5:10).

6

IF YOU ONLY KNEW THE GIFT

Let us look at another gospel scene, another encounter between Jesus and a sinner. This time we consider the meeting between Jesus and the Samaritan woman at the well of Jacob (Jn 4:5-42). As we read, let us remember that Jesus is God, revealing to us how God thinks and acts.

We know the story well. Jesus is on the road with some of his disciples and about noon they approach the Samaritan town of Sychar. Jesus is tired and thirsty and sits by the well of Jacob while the disciples go into the town to buy food. As Jesus sits and look down the road, he sees a lone figure coming towards the well. It is a Samaritan woman coming from the town to draw water. As the woman gets near she notices that the man at the well is a Jew and so she does not greet him since the two tribes are traditional enemies. She lowers the bucket into the deep well and as she pulls it up full of splashing fresh water, she is surprised to hear the stranger addressing her. He is thirsty and asks for a drink. The woman answers curtly: 'What! You a Jew and you ask me, a Samaritan, for a drink?' (Jn 4:9). The woman see only with her eyes. She misses the deeper reality of what is happening. 'You are a Jew. I am a Samaritan.' She does not know the hidden self of Jesus, nor her own hidden self. The reality is that Jesus is the Messiah and she is a person he loves and wants to bless. In his reply Jesus awakens her curiosity and hints that there is more here than meets the eye!

If you only knew what God is offering and who it is
that is saying to you; Give me a drink;
You would have been the one to ask and he would
have given you living water. (Jn 4:10)

How does the woman react to this? She is still only on the surface of the situation, seeing only the externals. The well is deep, this man has no rope, how can he give her water? She has not read the signs as Peter did. Jesus helps by rousing her curiosity and desire:

Whoever drinks this water will get thirsty again.
Anyone who drinks the water that I give, will never be thirsty again. (Jn 4:14)

Some kind of thirst is now awakened in her as she politely answers: 'Sir, give me some of that water.' Now Jesus has something important to do. He has to show the woman that he is aware of her sinful past so that she will not feel bad getting such a gift from this prophet when she is a sinner. So Jesus changes the conversation quite suddenly and says: 'Go and call your husband.' the woman answers, 'I have no husband.' Jesus praises her for telling the truth and shows that he knows all about her. But he does this in a gentle way. Remember what we said about true love. It does not make the other person feel small, or mean, or inferior. 'You are right to say, I have no husband; for although you have had five, the one you now have is not your husband. You spoke the truth there.' (v.18)

Note carefully some important points about the way Jesus treats this woman. Remember we are looking at God chatting with a sinner. When Jesus said earlier on, 'If you only knew who you were talking to', I feel the woman was probably saying to herself, 'And if you knew who you were talking to, you might not continue to chat!' Remember the scene in the house of Simon the Pharisee when Mary Magdalen gate-crashed and knelt before Jesus to kiss his feet. Simon was almost pleased, because for him this proved that Jesus was not a prophet, because in Simon's way of thinking Jesus would not allow such a woman to touch him. Even on this occasion, when the disciples returned from the town, they were shocked to find Jesus talking to this woman. The disciples here were thinking like Simon the Pharisee, thinking like you and me, perhaps, but not thinking like God. Let us learn from Jesus. Jesus did know the kind of woman he was talking to and that was why he was talking to her! The sick need the doctor. He had come to save and heal her.

Let us also notice that Jesus offered her the gift of living water, the gift of the Holy Spirit, before there was any question of her conversion. He said quite simply at the beginning of their meeting: 'If you knew the gift God has for you and who is talking to you, you would ask and he would give.' He offers her, a sinful woman, the all holy gift of the Spirit. The Spirit would teach the woman who she really was, the child of God. Knowing she was accepted and loved would give meaning to her life. She would be in touch with her hidden self, with reality, with God's love which would help her to grow, just as the tree planted by the stream is always nourished. No wonder, at the end of the encounter, that this woman ran back excitedly to the town to call out the people. She ran from door to door calling out 'Come and see a man who has told me all about myself.' (v.29)

Before leaving this scene, let us think for a moment about that woman before she met Jesus. Imagine her on the morning of that very day. She gets up to face another day. It would probably be true to say she was unhappy. From the story revealed by Jesus, she was a woman searching for love and happiness but never finding it. She had lived with five different men but none of the relationships had lasted. She was with a man now but did not have a settled relationship in a happy marriage. If she reflected on all this, she must have felt little hope of any change or improvement. It would always be the same. Her life was passing by with nothing to show. It was failure, waste and no likelihood of being anything different. So, she rises to face yet another day, just one more day, like all the others. Nothing would ever change. She picks up the rope and bucket to go to the well. She sets out, alone. This is significant. Was she cut off from the community in the town because of her bad reputation? Who would want the company of such a woman, who would want to talk to her? There was one person, who was not only willing to talk to her but ready to offer her a spring of living water, a treasure that would make all things new. He was waiting for her at the well. He was God.

7

TWO MEN ON TREES

There are two men in the gospel who met Jesus and experienced his salvation in rather unusual circumstances. When I think of one I always remember the other because they had some curious things in common. We know the name of one — Zacchaeus, but the other is known to us only as 'the good thief'. One thing they had in common was love of money. Zacchaeus was a kind of 'respectable thief'. He was a corrupt tax official and cheated within the law and so became very rich and remained free, though maybe not as free as people thought. The good thief was less respectable. He took money with violence and when he was caught, was sentenced to crucifixion. In the story of both, a tree plays a large part, though the two trees were very different!

Zacchaeus, we are told, was 'a wealthy man and a senior tax collector' (Lk 19:1-10). Tax collectors at that time were very unpopular because they used their job to get rich at people's expense. They paid a lump sum to Rome and then collected extra from the people to make an unjust profit. Zacchaeus was able to dodge the law but not his own conscience. He was not in prison but he was not free, he was not at peace, for we are told he wanted to see Jesus and indeed wanted it so much he took a terrible risk by climbing a tree! I don't mean the physical risk of falling and hurting himself, but the risk of being seen by the crowd and of being mocked. People would think it very strange to see a prominent and wealthy citizen up in a tree. Certainly Zacchaeus must have been very anxious to see Jesus.

Zacchaeus is very lucky because God has a sense of humour. When Jesus passes under the tree, he stops, looks up and calls Zacchaeus down with words which must have been wonderful in his ears, 'Zacchaeus, come down. Hurry, I must stay at your house today' (Lk 19:5-6). I wonder how did Jesus know his name! Zacchaeus must have nearly fallen out of the tree with joy. Here is a holy man different from the scribes and the Pharisees. they would not speak to him, unless maybe to insult and condemn him. Jesus wants not only to meet him but even to visit his home and family. We are told Zacchaeus 'welcomed him joyfully' (v.7). Let us notice that Jesus shows this love to Zacchaeus before there is any conversion. The love is unconditional, God's kind of loving, and of course it is not understood by many in the crowd. 'They all complained when they saw what was happening. He had gone to stay at a sinner's house, they said' (v.8). Our kind of loving is so small and petty. I think of the words of the landowner in the parable of the late workers, 'Why be envious because I am generous!' (Mt 20:16).

God knows what he is doing. Love is the best healing medicine. Love makes people new. Love brings out the best and reveals the deep hidden self. We are told: 'Zacchaeus said to the Lord. Look Sir, I am going to give half my property to the poor, and if I have cheated anybody, I will pay him back four times the amount' (v.8). Jesus finishes with a very gracious word: 'Today salvation has come to this house' (v.10). The blessing from Jesus is so great and rich that it overflows to the extended family of this little man who climbed a tree.

The other man we remember here is the good thief who was lifted up very unwillingly on to a very different kind of tree — the tree of the cross. But he too is so lucky, for God has let himself be lifted up on another tree, another cross, beside him, to that he can be near him. Zacchaeus was able to come down from his tree and meet Jesus and talk to him. They dying thief cannot come down but Jesus is glad to be lifted up beside him so they can talk. As Jesus had lived among sinners, so now will he die among them

37

and his own prophecy comes true: 'When I am lifted up from the earth, I shall draw all men to myself' (Jn 12:32).

So we stand on the hill of Calvary. Three men hang there on their crosses. One is God, hiding in Jesus. People stare curiously at them, laughing, mocking, insulting. Some, perhaps, are moved to pity. The end is near now. The sky is strangely dark as the sun appears to lose its light. Then one of the thieves with great effort and pain twists his head to look at Jesus, his fellow criminal. But this strange thief sees more than a criminal beside him. He does not judge with the eyes only. He reads the signs, he touches the reality hidden beneath the surface and speaks to Jesus: 'Jesus', he said, 'remember me when you come into your Kingdom' (Lk 23:42).

How we rejoice at this man's prayer and the faith it revealed. Surely his faith will save him. And how Jesus must have rejoiced too. Some of the leaders standing on the hill are shouting at him and mocking his claims to be a king, but here is a sinner friend believing and trusting. Jesus looks over at this new friend and says: 'Indeed, I promise you, today you will be with me in paradise' (v.43). Again, let us remember that we are listening to God speaking to a sinner. Today you will be in heaven. Today! Not tomorrow, not after thousands of days of purification, but this day, today. 'You will be with me.' Is that not in itself paradise, to be with Jesus? The last man Jesus spoke to on earth will be the first person to cross the threshold of heaven, hand-in-hand with Jesus his Saviour. The sinner and his friend Jesus.

I think again of Zacchaeus. He also got immediate blessings from Jesus beyond anything he expected. He had only hoped to see Jesus but instead Jesus wants to be a guest in his home. The good thief asked only to be remembered by Jesus in his Kingdom. Instead he is to enter the Kingdom immediately. Zacchaeus also heard the lovely word 'today'. Jesus said to him, 'Come down. Today I must stay at your house.' Zacchaeus was told to come down from the tree. The good thief can also come down from his tree of pain. Jesus wanted to go to the house of Zacchaeus; now Jesus wants to bring the good thief to his house, the heaven of God. Jesus was glad to go to the house of sinners while they lived. They, when they die with repentance and trust, are welcome in his Father's house.

8

A MEETING WITH JESUS

We have been looking at certain people in the gospel who met Jesus and had their lives transformed by him. Perhaps we envy them and feel how lucky they were. But, remember, as we said, God was hiding in Jesus and could only be seen with eyes of faith. Many others met Jesus and nothing happened because they did not have faith. Faith is always needed to find Jesus and to see God in him. Today we can, in our own way, meet Jesus through faith. One way is prayer. Every prayer is an act of faith. In prayer we can be with Jesus and talk to him and listen to him.

Here is a prayer exercise which may help you to meet Jesus. You need not fear your sins; Jesus won't chase you away. See how he accepted the sinful man, Peter. He won't make you feel guilty, no matter what you have done. See how gently he revealed her faults to the woman at the well. Your effort at prayer will be rewarded beyond your dreams. Zacchaeus hoped only to 'see' Jesus, but instead Jesus came and stayed in his house. The good thief asked only to be 'remembered' by Jesus when he reached heaven but instead he was escorted that very day into Paradise by Jesus himself. God always gives much more than we ask for or even hope for. Let us now seek this God in prayer. We ask the Holy Spirit to guide us and help us that we may experience the presence and healing power of Jesus.

One of the shortest parables told by Jesus in the gospels is one of my favourites and I want to suggest to you a prayer of the heart based on this parable.

> The Kingdom of Heaven is like a merchant looking for fine pearls; when he finds one of great value he goes and sells everything he owns and buys it.
>
> (Mt 13:45-46)

I want you to use your imagination as I lead you in this prayer. I ask you to imagine that you have received an important message from Jesus. He wants to meet you because he has something special to tell you.

Now try to imagine the place where you will meet Jesus. It should be a quiet place, a peaceful and beautiful place, maybe an actual place that you know which has nice memories for you or an imaginary place of peace and beauty. For example, it might be

> on a hillside overlooking a valley below
> or a cliff overlooking a lake
> it might be in a wood, a pleasant shady clearing
> in the forest
> or by a river bank, or in a garden or maybe even
> in a chapel
> which is quiet and empty.

Imagine now that you are in the place of your choice. You are sitting waiting for Jesus and wondering why he wants to see you, what is this special message he had for you. Then you look up and there is Jesus approaching; he is climbing up the hill to where you sit, or coming through the wood, or walking along the river bank, or entering the chapel and coming towards you.

> He is dressed as you imagine Jesus would be in
> his own traditional Jewish cloak
> or maybe in modern casual clothes as you think
> he might be in our time

> You welcome him and greet him in the way you
> think appropriate, with a handshake or a curtsy
> or an embrace

> Then you both sit down and Jesus is smiling and
> says

I'll bet you are wondering why I want to see you
and what message I have for you.

You nod your head, maybe a bit nervous as to
what the meeting and message might be about.

Then Jesus begins. He says:
First of all, I have something to show you.

He reaches inside his jacket and takes out a small
leather bag.

He opens and spills out on to his open palm a
large precious stone.

You gasp at its size and beauty.

You have never seen such a diamond.

It is like something alive as it glitters and shines
and flashes light of many colours in his hand.

It has many sides and edges for it has not yet
been cut into any particular shape

but its value is clearly immense and its beauty is
breath-taking.

Then Jesus looks intently at you
and he says: This precious stone is you,
            It stands for you.
I carry it to remind me of you.
Your beauty and value for me far outweigh
this stone.

This is what I wanted to tell you
to let you know how precious you are to me.

Do you remember the story I told about the
merchant searching for fine pearls?
I am that merchant and when I found you
I was ready to sell all to have your friendship
And that's what I did,
I gave everything — even my very life for you.
I feel just now that you have problems
and life is rough for you
and I felt I had to tell you this
how it is with me and you
hoping it would give you courage in time of
difficulty.
It was the thought of you and your friendship
that kept me going through my passion.

I hope the thought of me and my love for you
may help you through your suffering.
And you notice this precious stone has rough
edges;
It is not finally cut into shape yet;
that will take time,
but, believe me, I will be holding you all the time.
Some of life's experiences may hurt
but all the shaping and cutting is done with great
love
and above all I don't want to lose you.

Jesus puts the precious stone back in the leather bag and
returns it to his jacket. He offers his hands to you and
looks into your eyes and he says:

Trust me please.
Trust me that I am able to take care of you
for every single moment of your life.
You are never on your own;
I am with you all the time
And together we will cope

Now you tell him what is in your heart; it may be hard to find words but he reads every beat of your heart. Then after some chat, he gets up to leave. You embrace and then watch him go, climbing down the hillside, or making his way through the woods, or walking along the riverbank. Before he gets out of sight he turns and waves and you wave back.

9

BRING OUT THE BEST ROBE

We have been watching Jesus meeting certain people who like us were weak and sinful and had failed God. Jesus is God and we want to learn how God acts with us when we sin and fail. Does he stop loving us? Does he hold back his love until we have changed, until we have stopped sinning? We see clearly that this was not his way. Jesus always loves. God loves all the time. When Jesus met Peter, the woman at the well, Zacchaeus, the thief on the cross, how did he speak with them? Did he threaten them and try to frighten them into a change of heart? No! He accepted and loved them. It was this love which touched their hearts and changed them.

Then, in our prayer of the heart we imagined a meeting with Jesus. I hope you are able to accept the healing love he offered you, that you listened only to his voice telling you what you mean to him, revealing your true identity. Perhaps another voice was heard in your prayer, the voice of the tempter questioning the words of Jesus and trying to lead you into fear and self-hatred, telling you that you are unworthy and reminding you of your sins. Do not listen to this voice. The Father sent Jesus to us and tells us to listen to him. 'This is my son the beloved, listen to him' (Mt 17:5).

Someone once said to me, 'Father, do you not exaggerate in speaking as you do about God loving and accepting sinners? Is it not dangerous? It might give people a careless attitude to sin.' I could answer by saying that it is impossible to exaggerate when talking about God's love, it is always greater than I imagine.

But a better answer to that question comes from Jesus himself. Let us listen to it. It took the form of a story, the most famous short story in the Bible. Jesus tells the story to

45

answer those who were complaining that he was soft with sinners. Here is how St Luke introduces the story: 'The tax collectors and the sinners, meanwhile, were all seeking his company to hear what he had to say, and the Pharisees and the scribes complained. This man, they said, welcomes sinners and eats with them. So he spoke this parable to them' (Lk 15:1-3, 11-32).

Please read the story in your bible and remember, this is Jesus's own story. It is the fruit of his prayer and union with the Father. Jesus invented the plot and the different characters. He composed the dialogue and put the words into the mouths of the characters to bring out their different personalities. There are three major characters, a father and his two sons. Later editors of the Bible gave it a title: The Prodigal Son. The title misleads, in a way, because the central character is the Father. The whole purpose of the story was to reveal the Father who is God, and his compassion for human weakness and failure. We must prize this parable because here we are being given the inside story on God by the only one who knows. 'No one knows the Father except the Son and those to whom the Son chooses to reveal him' (Lk 10:22).

As you read the story, remember it is God's living word, ever fresh. Each time we read the story from the Scriptures it can teach us something new. Revelation is happening now. Let us concentrate on the father in the story. When his younger son asks for his share of the inheritance, the father gives it and, though he loves the boy dearly, he allows him to leave home. He allows the boy freedom. He will not force the boy to stay at home. God does not force us to love him. The boy travels to a far country, wastes the money, disgraces the family and ends up lonely, miserable and even starving. In his misery he thinks of home and his father — what a good father he had been. He decides to go home and say sorry and ask to be allowed to be a servant in his father's house since he is not fit to be a son. He sets out for home.

Notice what Jesus tells us about the father. Every word here is chosen by Jesus and full of meaning. First, Jesus tells us the father sees his son 'while he was still a long way off' (Lk 15:20). This is important. It means the father was watching out for the boy, hoping for his return. He was missing the boy and stood at the door each day, looking down the road. Then one day he sees a figure on the road, and even at a distance and despite the change in the boy, he recognises his son and Jesus tells us what was going on in his heart. 'His father saw him and was moved to pity' (v.20). If you ask me does God love you as you are and what does he think of you when you sin and then turn back to him, here is your answer. The father sees the boy, tired, worn, dirty, with ragged clothes, and he is 'moved to pity'. In his heart he is moved, his heart is moved with pity, not to anger, judgment or condemnation, but to pity.

The next incident in the story is almost incredible. We feel Jesus is exaggerating. He tells us, 'The father ran to the boy' (v.20). The father runs down to the road to welcome the boy. We would not expect this in any culture, that a parent should run to greet the young person, especially a young person who had disgraced him. But Jesus tells the story. God comes down the road to embrace the sinner.

When the father reaches the boy he embraces him and kisses him tenderly while the boy is trying to make his confession. 'Father, I have sinned against heaven and against you' (v.18). The father does not seem to be listening. He understands the human heart. The boy is back because he is sorry. Already the father is organising a celebration. Some servants had followed the old man down the road and the father is giving orders all over the place! 'Quick. Bring out the best robe and put it on him' (v.22). Notice every word. 'Quick.' Don't delay, don't let my son stand here in poverty. Bring out the robe, out here. No waiting to go inside and have a family council. Bring the best robe, not one of the second-hands. Don't forget the ring and the sandals. The poor boy's feet must be hurting

47

him! Call in the music-makers and go down to the farm and kill the best animal, that calf we have been fattening for the agricultural show. The boy is so thin. 'We are going to have a feast, a celebration, because this son of mine was dead and has come to life; he was lost and is found. And they begin to celebrate' (Lk 15:23-24).

And I am sure Jesus was rejoicing in his heart as he watched the faces in the listening crowd smiling, laughing, crying as they hear first-hand what God their Father was really like. These were moments Jesus treasured — when he was able to reveal to simple people the mystery of his Father's love. 'Many prophets and kings wanted to see what you see and never saw it; to hear what you heard and never heard it' (Lk 10:24). And elsewhere, Jesus cried out one day in praise: 'I bless you Father, Lord of heaven and of earth, for hiding these things from the learned and the clever and revealing them to mere children' (Mt: 11:25).

We might be tempted to say to Jesus, 'Your Father seems almost to be crazy.' Jesus would answer with a smile, 'My father and your father.' Indeed, God's love and compassion and forgiveness are somewhat crazy compared with our human love and forgiveness. This is what it means to be God.

How lucky we are to have such a God, such a Father. If it was a human father in the story would he not lecture the boy, remind him of his failure, demand an explanation and choose a suitable punishment? This father understands the human heart. He does not ask the boy why he acted that way. Is this not a favourite question among us? When a young person does wrong, what do most people ask the young offender? 'Why did you do it?' It is a hard question, for the young offender usually has no answer. He has no rational explanation for the evil that surfaced in his heart. God the Father spares the Prodigal Son that question.

Again, notice that the father asks for things only for the boy. He asks nothing from him. He asks for a robe, ring, sandals, music, food, all for the boy. Why? It's really very simple. He is his son and he loves him. All that matters is that he is safely home. This is the wonderful difference between human justice and the justice of God. When we fail in life and come before our peers, we are given what we deserve. When we fail and come before God, we are given what we need, namely love and healing forgiveness.

We cannot measure the love of God. We cannot measure the forgiveness of God. Sometimes we think God's love and God's forgiveness are like ours, only to an infinite degree. It is not so. God's love and forgiveness are like God himself, they are a mystery before which we should be lost in wonder. They are offered to us as gift. All we have to do is accept and we can become a new creation. We become new, not just cleansed. It is not that our sins are just washed away and we are made clean. They simply disappear as if they had never been committed and we are made new. St Paul, in the beautiful hymn to love, says: 'Love keeps no record of wrong' (1 Co 13:5). and St John tells us: 'God is love' (1 Jn 4:8). When we forgive, we find it hard to forget. We say we forgive, but then remind the other person of their failure and wrongdoing. We keep record of wrong. Maybe we don't write it down in a notebook, but it is in the mind. Not so with God.

Here is a humorous imaginary story to illustrate this point:

> A man died and arrived at heaven's gate. St Peter received him joyfully, giving him VIP treatment. Peter told him there was a special treat prepared for him on his first day. He was going to see a video! Peter went on to say it was a video of the man's whole life story from birth to death! The man did not feel too happy and wondered how Peter could call it a treat! Peter also said he would be watching the video with him. Then Peter set up the video and the film began. As it unfolded, the man noticed that

the film showed all the good things of his early life which he had forgotten, all the good deeds he had done as a boy, kind words and actions etc. And so it was all through the film right up to the end, none of his sins appeared. When it was over, he looked at Peter smiling and said, 'Peter, I think you have shown me a censored video.' But Peter answered, 'No, my friend. This is the real you. That's how we know you in heaven. Once a person is sorry, then the sin disappears and cannot be thought of again.'

10

SEVENTY-SEVEN TIMES

Let us go back again to the story of the father and his two sons. It didn't finish with the celebration for the prodigal's return. Jesus has more to teach us and he continues the story. He tells us that the elder boy was out working when his brother came home and was welcomed. We imagine this elder boy coming in from the fields. Like the young boy he also is tired and dirty, but from hard work on the farm. He hears music and laughter coming from the house and calls over a servant to ask what is happening. He is told: 'Your brother has come and your father has killed the calf we had fattened because he has got him back safe and sound' (Lk 15:27). Watch carefully now. Jesus has composed this story. Jesus has invented this character. Jesus knows the human heart. He describes the elder brother's reaction. 'He was angry then and refused to go in' (v.28). The father inside gets the message. What does he do? He does not say, 'Well it's up to him.' No, he loves this boy too, so, he leaves the party and comes out to ask the boy to come in.

The elder boy says to his father, 'Look, all these years I have slaved for you and never once disobeyed your orders, yet you never offered me so much as a kid for me to celebrate with my friends. But for this son of yours, when he came back after swallowing up your property — he and his women — you kill the calf we had been fattening' (vv.29-30). We can see from his words he is a strange boy, bitter, unhappy, with little love. He does not love his brother and won't forgive him. He does not even refer to him as brother but as 'this son of yours'. And it seems he didn't have much love for his father either. He looks on his father as a master for whom he works and from whom he expects rewards.

In all the parables of Jesus we are involved. Jesus is asking you and me here if we are like that. How do we see God our Father? Is he a master for whom I 'work'? Do I feel I must be 'good', I must keep commandments, I must work for God to earn his rewards? But this is not the kind of relationship God wants. God is not master. He is Father. We are not servants. We are children, we are family. The young prodigal thought that because of his sins he could no longer be son and should become servant, but the father would not hear of it. God's love is given to us not as a reward which we can earn by good deeds but is given as a gift, as love, because we are his. Notice the words used by the Father to try to explain the situation to this elder boy: 'My son, you are with me always and all I have is yours. But it was only right we should celebrate and rejoice, because your brother here was dead and has come to life, he was lost and is found' (vv.31-32).

What wonderful words! They are spoken to you and to me: 'You are always with me. All I have is yours.' God says that to me. He gives me everything. He shared his very life with us in creation, then gave us his Son who thought us worth dying for and invited us into his family through baptism and tells us his home is our home. Heaven is our home. It is not a reward for being good. It is our home. Maybe some may not choose to go in like the elder brother sulking in the yard and refusing to join the party. But that is not God's fault.

Why did the elder boy not forgive his younger brother? I don't know. Was it jealousy, anger, selfishness? I don't know. But by refusing to forgive and love his brother he cut himself off from the celebration.

We have been reflecting on God's love for us and his acceptance of us. We have also looked at our failure and the ugly side of ourselves, our sinfulness, and have seen that God can cope with that. He forgives and heals and forgets when we go back to him and say sorry. Now Jesus, at the end of his story, leads us into a new truth, namely, if

I am to experience this healing forgiveness, if I am to be able to celebrate to the full with my Father, I, in turn, must be like my Father and I must love and forgive others. The elder boy is outside in the yard because he won't forgive his brother. Is there some of that elder boy in me? Yes, of course there is. Some of that unforgiving spirit is in all of us. We all find it hard to forgive. St Peter was troubled by this and one day asked Jesus: 'Lord, if someone offends me, how often must I forgive him? Would seven times be enough?' We know the answer Jesus gave. 'Not seven times, Peter, but seventy-seven times' (Mt 18:22). What Jesus means here is that we must always forgive. And if we were to ask Jesus why we should always forgive, he would say: 'Because your Father always forgives you.' If we really believe that God forgives us in the way we described, that he keeps no record of wrong, then we should find here the power to forgive each other.

God's forgiveness of us and our forgiveness of each other are two sides of one coin. We cannot have one without the other. Jesus put it bluntly: 'If you don't forgive each other your Father won't forgive you' (Mt 6:15). This is not a threat. Jesus does not threaten. This is a statement of reality. We cannot love God and hate our brother. If our love is genuine it must include God and our brethren. We cannot experience God's forgiveness, really experience it, and at the same time refuse to share it with others and forgive them.

If at the moment you are finding it hard to forgive someone I would ask you to consider seriously whether you really believe that you are right now totally forgiven by God. We will return to this in the next chapter but let us close here with a true story of a great example of human forgiving which may give us courage.

In Holland during the Second World War there lived a Christian family called ten Boom. Their little country was invaded by Germany and immediately the

Nazi anti-Jewish campaign began. Jews were rounded up and transported to the death camps in Germany. The ten Boom family were full of compassion for the suffering Jews and risked their lives to save as many Jews as possible. They built a secret room in their house over the shop where the father of the family worked as a watch seller. When Jews came to the shop, the family would offer to help them escape. They would hide the Jewish families in the secret room and smuggle them out at night over the border.

Then the terrible thing happened. Someone reported the family to the Nazi authorities. The Gestapo arrived in trucks and the whole family was dragged out and sent to the camps in Germany where they died after much brutal treatment — all except one daughter, Corrie. Despite her terrible suffering Corrie remained strong in her Christian faith and always had a very special trust in God the Father. She saw members of her family die, but due to some clerical accident in the camp she was released.

When the War ended she devoted herself to evangelisation and wrote many books. She stressed the theme of Christian love and forgiveness. Many years later she was back in Germany addressing very large audiences on the Christian faith. One day after a rally she was told that a man wished to see her urgently. When the man came she noticed that he was very disturbed. He told Corrie that he had found Jesus in his life but he would have no peace till she forgave him. Corrie answered that there must be a mistake since she had never seen him before and so there could be nothing to forgive. Now the man began to cry and confessed that he was the person who had betrayed her family to the Nazi authorities during the War. He held out his hand to ask her forgiveness.

Corrie tells us that when she heard the confession her mind was flooded with all the horrible memories of the brutal deaths of her family. And even though she had just preached about forgiveness, she was not able to lift her hand to give this man the sign of reconciliation. She felt as if her arm was paralysed. She just stood there. After some moments she heard the voice of God the Father speaking in her heart, reminding her that he had forgiven her everything in her life and always would. The loving image of God gently pushed away the other terrible images from the War. She felt the blood flow in her arm and was able to give her hand to this man as a sign of forgiveness.

Where did Corrie get the power to forgive this man? Not from her own human resources alone, but from God present within her, reminding her of his forgiveness and empowering her to be like him. Forgiving involves letting go, letting go the past, letting go images and memories. We can become almost paralysed by small offences and we hold on to them. No! Please let them go and let God heal you. Let go and let God take over — you will be as free as a bird in the sky and you will experience healing.

11

ALL IS GIFT

I believe if we really experience God's forgiveness, experience it not just with our minds but with our hearts, then we will find the power to forgive one another. Let us consider one of our Lord's parables which may help us to have that experience. It is the parable of the late workers in the vineyard. Read it in your bible, Matthew 20:1-16.

In this parable a farmer goes out to hire workers for his vineyard. He hires some men at the start of the day and they agree on a fair wage. Throughout the day he hires other men at different hours, bringing in some workers just before the end of the working day. At the end of the day he pays the same wage to all the workers, those who started early and those who came in at the end of the day. Naturally, those who had started early complained.

This parable always puzzled me and even annoyed me because I felt the farmer was unfair. But now the story helps me greatly.

The first mistake I made was that I stood, as it were, outside the parable and judged it just as a story. I did not feel personally involved and to me it seemed unfair that the late workers should get the same pay as the early ones. I was reading the story like an item of news in the daily paper and complaining about the treatment of the early workers.

Then I realised I was not supposed to be outside the parable, reading it like a judge. I was supposed to be inside the story and the story was to judge me! Jesus told his parables about me, about you, about all of us. We are the characters in the parables. When we accept this, Jesus is able to teach us deep truths about ourselves, about the nature of God and about our relationship with God and each other.

So then, I put myself into the parable, but I confess I still felt the farmer was in some way unfair. I was still complaining about his strange 'generosity'. It was at this stage that God blessed me. He opened my eyes and showed me how blind I had been. He showed me that the reason why I was still annoyed with the farmer was that I was identifying myself with the wrong characters in the story!

I was identifying myself with the early workers. Naturally this made me envious of the late workers getting the same pay. But now I felt Jesus asking me: 'Is that where you belong? Have you always been faithful to me in love? Have you lived totally and unselfishly for me since the morning of your lifetime?' When I tried to answer these questions, I had to face my poverty and sinfulness. I now began to see how good, patient and merciful God had been to me and I began to rejoice in his generosity. God had given me everything, my life and all his love and forgiveness, even though I had in no way earned these. He gave me everything because he is love and truly loves me. Everything I have is gift.

My true place in this parable is with the latest of the late workers. How could I or indeed anyone earn the love of God? Did I create my own life? How could I pay for a share in God's own life? What price could I pay for my salvation? The truth is, we cannot pay, we cannot earn these blessings. God's love and my salvation are gift, or 'grace', which is the scripture word for gift. It is the 'amazing grace' we sing of. 'It is by grace that you have been saved, through faith; not by anything of your own, but a gift from God; not by anything you have done, so that nobody can claim the credit' (Ep 2:8-9).

By identifying with those early workers, I was making myself like the elder brother in the parable of the prodigal son. I was thinking like that boy and not like the father in the story. Like him I was looking on God as my master. I work for him by trying to keep his commandments. If I succeed, he must reward me. If someone else does not work as hard as me, he should get less from God. If some-one comes in late in the day like the prodigal son, there should be no party for him. He has not earned it. But this is not the language of love, not the language of the father. It is the language of calculation and measurement, of reward and punishment. God does not speak this lan-guage, but I had been wanting him to do so. I was trying to change God, to make him a God of contract and not covenant, to make him small like myself. The words of the farmer in the parable were really meant for me: 'Why be envious because I am generous?' (Mt 20:16).

In telling this parable, Jesus had the scribes and Phar-isees in mind. They obscured the love and generosity and forgiveness of God. It is always a temptation for religious people to presume that they know God and to measure his generosity and reduce him to human size. Jesus was angry with such pride which made a travesty of his beloved Father. He told the scribes and Pharisees bluntly: 'You do not know me nor do you know my Father' (Jn 8:19).

The scribes and Pharisees had obscured the gift of God and the God of gift. They were restricting God's freedom to bestow his gifts as he pleases. They had substituted the God of contract and law. By their attitude to sinners they encouraged the idea that law comes first and then God's love is offered as a reward for observing the law. Jesus came to reverse this way of thinking. God gave his love before he gave laws. He chose the Jewish people, not because they were good or great, but because he had set his heart on them (Dt 7:7-8). First he stepped into their his-tory and saved them from Egypt. He then made his covenant with them and gave them the law which was joyfully welcomed by the people as a sign of their accep-tance of the covenant and a way of loving God and each other. Jesus came to restore love as the ultimate reality and the first commandment.

The parable of the late workers invites me to reflect on how I see God and what kind of God I worship. Can I honestly put myself among the late workers and believe that I who am so unworthy have been given all of God's favour, that everything is gift, that any goodness in me is God's work? Without Jesus I would be lost. But Jesus my saviour has come and endured suffering and death to bring me forgiveness, freedom, life, hope.

If I could realise this with my heart, I would be excited. I might be like Mary Magdalen in the gospel story. You remember how she rushed joyfully into the unwelcoming house of Simon the Pharisee and wept tears of joy over the feet of Jesus. She loved much because she knew she was forgiven much. Think of Jesus' words to Simon on that occasion: 'He loves little who is forgiven little' (Lk 7:17). That was my problem. I seemed to think I had little to be thankful for.

When we see we have everything to be thankful for, when we see God's love, life, forgiveness, heaven as pure gift, given to be shared with others, then we may begin to see each other in a new light and begin to relate to each other in a more God-like way and be more ready to forgive. This power to love and forgive others is also God's gift.

12

GOD IS PATIENT

We continue to reflect on the mystery of God and our own self and our relationship with God. We want it to be a relationship of love. We believe he loves us and we want to love him. What kind of God are we talking about, what kind of love?

Here is a humorous story which may help us to reflect on these matters.

> One day in heaven God decided to take a stroll through his paradise. He was surprised to find such a large population and began to worry about overcrowding. He called Peter and asked how so many got in to heaven. Peter reminded him about his own teaching that we must always forgive! But God was worried about overcrowding and told Peter to bring him the file on the ten commandments and assemble all the people! God then spoke to the great crowd and said he had heard that some had got in under false pretences. He would now read out the commandments one by one and after each commandment those who had broken that law would have to leave and go to 'the other place'. So, God began to read and after each commandment a large number got up sorrowfully and headed for heaven's gate. This went on up to the tenth commandment and after it was read everyone had left except one man. He was a man who had led a very righteous life.
> But God was now very unhappy and looked at Peter and said: 'This is terrible, heaven will now be cold and lonely. It's not good for man to be alone.' And with that God changed his mind. He told Peter to

run down to the gate and see if the people had left. Peter reported back that the buses had not yet come and the people were all standing in queues. God was very happy and forgave everyone and called them all back to the joy of heaven.

But now the one man who had been left, when he heard this decision, jumped up and shouted. 'That is unfair. If I had known that I would have lived differently!'

What kind of 'love' did that man have for God? Could we call it love at all? He kept commandments and laws not out of true love but to get a reward. He clearly did not love the others whom God called to share his heaven. He did not want their happiness, but only his own. Is it not like the elder boy in the story of the prodigal son? Is he not like the early workers in the parable of the landowner and his vineyard? This person is like the Pharisee. He observes law to have a reward and he wants only judgment for others who are weak. The sinner should get what he deserves. Jesus condemned such people in very strong language because they were giving such a false idea of God the Father. And he accused them saying: 'You will not allow others to go into heaven' (Mt 23:13).

Our God is patient. Our God is understanding. Don't we always want others to be understanding with us? In pre-marriage instruction classes we discuss with engaged couples the qualities that they like or dislike in a partner. The most popular quality, the one most desired is, 'understanding'. I would like my partner to be understanding. Why is this? I think it is because we know ourselves well. We know that at times we will fail, will do foolish things, things which indeed we ourselves don't understand. It is at times like this that we desperately hope our partner will understand. All through Scripture God uses the image of marriage to describe his love relationship with us. He is our divine partner and he is infinitely understanding.

And God is patient, so patient with our human weakness. He loves and waits and hopes the sinner will return. There is no sudden condemnation with God, no instant judgment. We are so lucky. He waits for us. He wants our healing, our salvation. What a great pity we are not patient with each other. Very often religious people who have kept God's law or who have experienced some kind of conversion can become intolerant of human weakness in others. They have no patience. They judge others and want God to judge them, now! They seem to forget that God waited for them. Should they not rejoice that God now waits for others?

Jesus told another parable about this. And again this parable seems shocking to some people (Mt 13:24-30). The farmer sows good grain in his field. But, at night, an enemy sows weeds. When the workers see the weeds they want to root them out immediately. The master says no, wait for the harvest. This parable is about the patience of God. Jesus told the parable because he knows the heart of man. He knows the temptation to pride and self-righteousness which is built in to all religion. He saw how the scribes and Pharisees prayed and fasted but were far from God and warned that tax collectors and prostitutes would enter heaven before them. They kept the law but despised those who failed. This is false religion. False because it suggests that I can be good by my own efforts. Those who think that go on to believe that they are a spiritual success and can claim heaven as a just reward, despising others who fail to observe the laws. Such people want to belong to a sin-free Church of the pure, the sinless who wish to sort out the saved before God's time. The servants in the parable are more zealous than the master for a weed-free field. They want the weeds out immediately. The master is more patient.

In your Christian life don't compare yourself with others. Thank God for his love and forgiveness, accept and share these with others, keep trying your best, be sure that without him you can do nothing. Criticise yourself, not others. Speak like St Paul: 'I hope to take my place in the resurrection of the dead. Not that I have become perfect yet. I have not yet won, but am still running, trying to capture the prize for which Christ Jesus captured me. I can assure you, my brothers, I am far from thinking I have already won. All I can say is that I forget the past and I strain ahead for what is still to come' (Ph 3:11-14).

Let us try to imitate St Paul, to keep trying and striving in the Christian life. Elsewhere, Paul says it is something that has to grow. There is no instant holiness. Jesus' favourite image for the Kingdom was a seed. Paul prays for his fellow Christians, for 'their hidden self to grow'. (Ep 3:16). Growth is slow and God is patient like any good farmer or gardener. In the parable of the vine Jesus says, 'My Father is the gardener' (Jn 15:1). When a farmer plants the grain of corn he can already in his mind see the green stalk and full corn cob as if it were hiding in the little seed. Because of this he will work hard to protect its growth. A good gardener knows that this tiny dry seed can become a flower with great beauty of shape, colour, perfume. Because he believes this, he will water and protect the seed and tend it with great care. God looks on us and knows we can become what he has created us to be.

We receive a new life when we accept Jesus and his Kingdom. Jesus says it is like being born again. But we know when a baby is born that it has to grow. Its whole life's work is to grow as a Christian person. Waiting for growth calls for patience. We must be patient with ourselves and with each other as God is patient.

13

WHO WANTS RUBBISH?

In the story of the Prodigal Son Jesus shows us how well he understands the human heart. When the younger son had messed up his life, wasted all his money and was reduced to misery and hunger, he felt lonely, sad and guilty within himself. He was heavily burdened with his sin. What could he do? Fortunately, he took the right step and decided to go back to his father and confess. His father was the only one who could take away this burden. 'I will leave this place and go to my father and say: "Father I have sinned against heaven and against you"' (Lk 15:18). Jesus understands our hearts. He knows that no one wants to carry round the burden of sin and guilt in their heart. It is rubbish. We want to get rid of it. Who wants to leave rubbish lying around their house? It brings disease, even death. We burn rubbish or put it outside the house to be collected by the rubbish van. Why hold on to the rubbish of our sins?

It is interesting to see the customs in different cultures which express this deep truth about people — that they don't want to carry evil or sin around in their hearts. Before the time of Jesus and the Sacrament of Reconciliation which he gave us, the Jews had the ceremony of the scapegoat. The people of a village would gather in a public place, form a circle and put a goat in the centre. The priest of the village would then pray and call down on the head of the goat all the sins of the village. After this, the people drove the unfortunate animal out into the desert. The goat symbolically carried away the sins from the people and was not allowed to return (Lv 16:20-22).

In some tribes in Kenya people who were burdened with guilt went to a good witchdoctor. To be set free from the burden of guilt they would confess the evil they had done. As they confessed they were given a container of water. They did not swallow the water but spat it out into a hole in the ground. This hole was then covered and in this way their sins were 'buried' and they were free.

In Thailand the people of a village come together and pray for the forgiveness of their sins. They then go down to the river bank. There they make little boats from the leaves of river plants. They 'wish' their sins on to these little boats which are then pushed out into the swift current which carries them away.

We are dealing here with something deep in our human make-up. It is this. We are not made for evil. We are made for good, to seek good and rejoice in it. When we go against the good, when we cooperate with evil and do wrong we are ill at ease. We feel guilty. We are our own first judge. We want to be freed from the guilt and the strange sadness it brings. God's holy Spirit working in our good hidden self moves us to renounce the evil; we crave a sign that the evil has been taken away and the guilt removed, and we are free again.

God knows all this and in Jesus he has given to the Christian village, the Christian community, a sign, a sacrament, a chance to say sorry, to renounce the evil, to get rid of the rubbish, to hear his pardon pronounced and to experience the healing forgiveness. All these blessings are found in the Sacrament of Reconciliation. Some who do not understand the Catholic sacrament say: 'Why tell my sins to a priest? Only God forgives sin and sets us free from guilt. It's enough to tell God'. It is true that only God forgives and sets free from guilt. It is also true that I must tell God the evil and say sorry to him. But through Jesus and the sacrament God has given us a wonderful way of doing this, a way which answers the deep need of our heart for some external sign which reassures us that our repentance is accepted and that we are forgiven and free. A Catholic does not say sorry to the priest. He says sorry to God in the presence of his brother, God's priest, and through that brother in faith hears God's forgiving, healing words. And the first words of that healing prayer spoken by the priest remind the forgiven sinner that the healing and freedom experienced are the gift of our heavenly Father given through the power of his Holy Spirit and made possible by the love of Jesus revealed in his passion, death and resurrection. The sacramental prayer begins:

> God, the Father of mercies, through the death and resurrection of his Son, the Lord Jesus, has saved the world and sent the Holy Spirit to us for the forgiveness of our sins.

This prayer reminds us of a central truth of the Christian faith, that we are saved through the death and resurrection of Jesus. We are familiar with this truth which often comes up in Scripture and in prayers and hymns. St Paul says Jesus died for our sins. By his death we are saved (1 Co 15:3). As this is such an important matter and one that could be misunderstood, we will consider it at length in the next chapter.

But just now let us thank God for being so patient with us, for being so understanding of our weakness by giving us the Sacrament of Reconciliation. Let us show our appreciation of the gift by using it. Let us learn from our brother the Prodigal Son. In prayer and sacrament let us arise and go back to our Father and confess our failure. If we do, be sure that we will experience our heavenly Father running down the road to welcome us.

And one last thing. As your Father forgives you completely, you must forgive yourself completely. God forgets about the past. You must do the same. You will not have the full, joyful, healing experience of God's forgiveness if you do not forgive yourself. Some people lose the value of God's forgiveness by refusing to forgive themselves. They go on punishing themselves. I believe if we act like this, then we have not really believed that we are forgiven. When we realise with our whole heart that God really has forgiven and forgotten then I think we will be excited. We will forgive ourselves and others too. This is healing.

But some lose this blessing. Even after confession they continue to feel bad and blame themselves. They continue to think about past sin and failure. Sometimes this may even be pride and not repentance. They may be more upset at letting themselves down before others than at failing God. True repentance lets go. When God has forgiven, then the sin no longer exists. So we too must let go. You cannot hold on to something that does not exist!

Sometimes in a retreat people write out their sins on papers which they then burn in a ceremony of repentance. This again is an expression of that desire we spoke of, the need for an external sign by which I renounce the sin and it is removed from me. When these papers are burnt there is nothing left, only a light, flaky paper ash. Throw this up into the wind and it is broken, dissolved, scattered, and cannot be gathered up again. The ash has disappeared. Our forgiven sins have as much reality as that scattered ash. They have been burnt to nothing in the fire of God's love. Let us forget as our God does. Let us not waste time regretting the past. We must get on with living and loving.

14

OTHER WOUNDS

We all need the healing forgiveness of our sins. But there are other wounds besides our sins. There is much pain and suffering in life that has little to do with sin and moral failure and we all need to be healed of these hurts and wounds as well. Nobody escapes these hurts. Your friend who appears calm and peaceful may be very wounded and in great need of healing. What kind of hurts do I mean? Here are some examples of the sufferings of life that affect very many people.

I was unjustly dismissed from my job years ago. I fell in love with someone who did not love me and who went off with another person. My parents separated and my stepparent shows me no love. My father is an alcoholic and mistreats Mum and us kids. I offended someone badly years ago and would love to apologise but the person is dead. My brother is drinking and on drugs and is breaking Mum's heart. My wife has cancer. In our family I always get the worst things; my brother is very clever and he gets the best; my sister is very pretty and she gets the best. My husband has AIDS. I always feel so lonely. I am impotent. I have never known my natural father. I am crippled with shyness. I feel I was never wanted by my parents. The list can go on and on.

Such suffering can be more painful than any physical suffering. I have often heard others say what I myself have felt when subject to some of this pain. 'I would rather have a broken arm or a dose of flu than endure such emotional pain.' These hurts wound our spirit. They can be like poison in our soul. They blot out the sunshine of life and rob us of happiness. They prevent us growing to become the people God wants us to be.

Do you think Jesus cares about these sufferings and hurts? Do you think he can do anything about them? Can he heal them? Of course Jesus cares. Anything that hurts you is his concern. He loves you. You are his and he wants your peace and happiness and growth. Did he not say, 'I have come so that they may have life and have it to the full' (Jn 10:10).

He wants you to experience healing and growth, new life and beauty, so you can share with others. He wants you to be a channel of his love, peace and happiness for others. Jesus cares more than you realise. And, of course, he can do something. 'It is not those who are well who need the doctor, but the sick' (Lk 5:31). Jesus is that doctor who has come to heal not just sins, not just illness, but the whole person. Jesus is like the Good Samaritan who will not pass you by when you lie hurt and wounded by the roadside of life. He stops, comes over, kneels beside you, pours soothing oil and binds up your wounds.

In one gospel scene we are told that Jesus was teaching one Sabbath in the Synagogue. He saw a woman in the crowd with a painful deformity. 'She was bent double and quite unable to stand upright' (Lk 13:12). Now this poor woman had been suffering like that for eighteen years. Imagine not being able to stand up straight for that long! Jesus notices and is moved to pity. 'When Jesus saw her he called her over and said, "Woman, you are rid of your infirmity", and he laid his hands on her. And at once she straightened up and she glorified God' (Lk 13:12-13). The official in the Synagogue was angry because the cure was made on the Sabbath and he scolded the people and told them not to come for healing on the Sabbath! 'But the Lord answered him. "Hypocrites", he said, "Is there one of you who does not untie his ox or his donkey from the manger on the Sabbath and take it out for watering? And this woman, a daughter of Abraham, whom Satan had held bound these eighteen years — was it not right to untie her bonds on the Sabbath day?"' (Lk 13:15-17).

Are we not all in some way like this poor woman? We are bound, tied, restricted by different chains and bonds which we ourselves cannot untie. We are bowed down by burdens and weights which prevent us standing up straight and being free. Perhaps we are in that condition for many years, even for eighteen years, maybe even for a longer time. Can we be free? Yes. Can the bonds be untied and the burden be lifted? Yes, Jesus can do it and wants to do it. 'Is it not right that this daughter of God, this son of God should be untied and set free?' What must we do? We have very little to do. Jesus sees us and knows our hurt and calls us over as he calls the woman. Let us go to him so that he can touch us.

You know the lovely hymn we often sing, 'Just a Closer Walk'. In that beautiful hymn we say that we long to walk more closely with the Lord. What does that mean? It means not merely to be physically closer to Jesus but to deepen the friendship between us, to keep close in love because he cares. 'When I falter, Lord, who cares?' Is it not Jesus? We speak of walking with Jesus and mostly we think of this walk as a walk into the future. But there is another very important walk we can make with Jesus, and that is a walk back into the past. Indeed, Jesus is the only one who could make such a walk with us. Jesus is God. He is not tied by time. So he can walk with you back down the past years of your life, even right back to childhood.

Invite him to do this with you. Put your hand firmly into his and walk close together back down the years. As you do, you will meet some of those painful happenings, some of those unhappy situations when you were hurt badly. Don't run away from the memory. Relive it again. There is no need to be afraid. Jesus holds your hand, he puts his arm around your shoulder. Let the painful memory come but keep close to Jesus. You hear the angry, hurtful words that were spoken, you see the cold, scornful look, you feel the pain again. But now Jesus is talking and saying, 'Don't be afraid. I understand. I love you. I am with you. I was with you on that day long ago but you were too upset to realise. Let me touch this wound. I want to heal it. It's all right now. Surrender it all to me now. Accept the peace I give you. Hand over the hurt and pain. I want to take it from you. Together let us forgive this person or those people. They did not know what they were doing. Forgive now. It's all in my hands. Now you are free. You can stand up straight now. This is what I came to do for you.' 'If the Son makes you free, you will be free indeed' (Jn 8:36).

Another way to experience Jesus' healing help in these matters is to invite Jesus to come with you on an inner journey into yourself. Jesus says to you what he said to Zacchaeus, 'I must stay at your home today' (Lk 19:16). Invite Jesus to walk with you as he did with Zacchaeus, invite him into your heart, your house. As you make the inner journey you come together to a room marked 'Memory'. You stand before the door afraid to open it because inside are many painful things, angry words, rejection, neglect, injustice, fears, jealousy, insults. He says there is nothing to fear as he has power over everything in the room. So you open the door for him and you go in together and his presence brings a flood of light into the room and everything looks different now in the light, just as at dawn we see that the dark, threatening, waving object that terrified us in the dark of night is only a tree blowing in the wind.

Jesus moves around the room and lays his hands gently on everything as he so often gently touched so many sick people and their wounds. As he touches ugly things they become clean and healed as did the skin of the leper which he gently touched; they cease to be twisted and become straight like the back of that daughter of Abraham who was bound for eighteen years; things that were dark become bright, the way the eyes of the blind man lit up with new light when Jesus touched them. As you walk around with Jesus on this healing walk his understanding and love and power are so great that it affects you deeply and you know all is well.

So from things that were dark and ugly comes new life, healing, beauty. God can do this. Is he not doing it all the time with the seeds we plant in our gardens? What a poor little thing a seed can be, with no beauty of shape or appearance, but out of this little misshapen object our God can bring a beautiful flower, beautiful in design, colour and perfume. Nothing is impossible with our God.

The Good News is that Jesus is alive and with us and ever busy among us always working, saving, healing. The Good News is not something that happened many years ago in Palestine. It is happening now. 'Today I want to go to your house' (Lk 19:16). 'Today as you listen these words are fulfilled' (Lk 4:22). With God it is always today. God never rests from loving. Remember how angry Jesus was with the Synagogue official for telling the people they should not seek a cure on the Sabbath. God takes no day of rest from curing. On another occasion when Jesus healed a sick man on the Sabbath the religious leaders blamed and scolded Jesus. How did he defend himself? His answer to them was, 'My Father goes on working and so do I' (Jn 5:17). There is no Sabbath from loving.

So Jesus is eager to heal us of all these painful, hurtful memories. He wants to make us whole, to give us fullness of life. Come to him in prayer, come trustingly like children. Indeed, many of our hurts go back to childhood. Now we are adults but inside many adults there is a hurt child. Jesus said, 'Suffer the children to come to me. Don't stop them.' We come in prayer. Prayer is his activity more than ours. He puts his arms around us and blesses us as he did the children long ago. Believe that his healing power can reach back to the past. Open the door of Memory for him. Evil is not irreversible. Don't say 'What's done cannot be undone.' Nothing is impossible to Jesus. He can heal the past and bring peace. Accept the healing and stand up straight again and with that daughter of Abraham glorify God (Lk 13:13).

15

HE DIED FOR MY SINS

One of the central truths of the Christian faith is that in Jesus Christ our sins are forgiven and we are given new life. In him we become a new creation. From the very beginning this has been the faith and teaching of the Church. It is usually expressed by saying 'Christ died for us. Christ died for our sins.' Paul writes to the Romans: 'He not only died for us but he rose from the dead and now pleads for us before the Father' (Rm 8:34). Then we have the wonderful words of Jesus himself: 'A man can have no greater love than to lay down his life for his friends' (Jn 15:13). Each of us can say with total truth, 'Jesus Christ gave his life for me, his friend.' This is the great love story between God and us and should be the source of all our joy, hope, courage and love.

Let us think about this. What does it mean to say 'Jesus died for my sins'? I think it is easy to go wrong here and misunderstand this teaching. If not understood properly it could lead to fear and new guilt instead of joy, peace and love. How we understand the Christian truth, 'Jesus died for my sins', will depend on how we understand and interpret what happened on Calvary. And this in turn depends very much on how we understand God. What kind of God do we believe in?

As we grow up our ideas develop and change. Our idea of God will surely change as we move through the different stages and experiences of life. My idea of God has changed a great deal since I was a boy. In those days I thought God was very far away, living in the clouds. He created me for heaven, which was nice, but I had to prove myself: I had to be tested. If I kept his laws I would pass and be rewarded with heaven. If I failed seriously I would be punished in hell. This God saw everything I did, even in the dark. He noted it all down in a book which would be read out on the last day. But this God had pity on me. He saw that I could not pay the price for my sins. So he sent his Son to save me. The Son also had pity on me and, as it were, took my place in the dock. Judgment was passed by God on his Son. Then, on a cross, the Son paid the price for my sins. Calvary was the place of punishment. Jesus was punished. I was set free. So, Jesus died for my sins. I don't really know if someone told it to me exactly like that but that was how I believed it.

Today I believe that this is a false image of God and a distortion of the true meaning of Calvary. The God I imagined in my childhood was not the God revealed by Jesus. The Father revealed by Jesus in the story of the Prodigal Son is the true God. Can we imagine that Father punishing his Son with the Cross? If we see Calvary as punishment, then God the Father becomes a tyrant handing out a brutal punishment to his innocent and beloved Son. If his anger had to be satisfied in that way, we can only now live in fear and with a new sense of guilt since we are responsible for the death of Christ. And what kind of peace or joy could we have, knowing so well our human weakness and tendency to sin again?

It is not enough for us to get rid of a false idea of God and Calvary. We must be able to understand the true picture in some way. I say 'in some way' because we can never fully understand the wisdom and power of God revealed on Calvary. This is still the heart and centre of my faith. But in what way can we understand it? I think we cannot begin to understand it until we accept Calvary as a love story. The key to any understanding here is love. Many saints have said that what kept Christ on the cross was not nails and ropes but love. Although Calvary is connected with sin and evil, it is not a place of punishment but a place of love, the love of the Blessed Trinity.

God the Father saw the suffering of his people in the world just as he had seen the suffering of his Chosen People in Egypt. In Egypt the oppressor was Pharaoh. Now the oppressor is the sin in people's hearts, a human selfishness which often refuses to go out in love to others. Men and women seem trapped in their human weakness and failure. They are alienated from God and each other and because of guilt and fear in the human heart they are alienated from their own best selves. People could not save themselves, could not heal themselves. God so loved his people that he sent his Son to them in their predicament. They could not believe in themselves and were losing a sense of their own identity. The Son came to help people to believe in themselves, to heal them by helping them to rediscover their true identity.

Jesus came with a message and he called it Good News. The message, the Good News was:

> You are still God's people. He still loves you with an everlasting love. He has not given up on you because of your failure. He does not despise you because of your sin. He is still on your side. He is not far away but among you. He is active among you, healing, liberating, recreating you. All these things he has been telling you through many prophets but now he is among you himself in me, doing all these things. Believe this message, this Good News, and accept me, and the power of the Spirit will come on you. In that power turn to one another, forgive and be reconciled to each other. Do away with anger and injustice and live as God's family.

This message, which Jesus not only preached but lived out in his love for the poor and the sinner, provoked strong opposition among the influential religious leaders. They were angry at his disregard for the Sabbath and other sacred traditions. They were furious because he challenged their pride and lack of mercy. Above all they were incensed that he claimed to be doing all this in God's name and as God's representative, equal in some way to God.

As months passed by, the opposition grew and it became clear to Jesus that these men could injure, even destroy him. Jesus knew the fate of unpopular prophets. With the passing of time Jesus saw he would have to make a definite choice if he wished to avoid danger and save his life. He would either have to give up his message and life-style and thus save his life or continue preaching and living the Good News and thus risk his life. But he could not change the message or stop preaching it. This was what the Father sent him to do and he could only teach what he heard from the Father. He would die if necessary in order that the good news from the Father should be preached. He had to convince men and women that God was serious about his love, he had to prove that love was powerful enough to cope with any evil, even death. He was not only preaching and living love but inviting us to accept the love and use it to overcome our sinful selfishness towards each other. So, he gave us the supreme example. He made his choice. He would die for what he believed in, for love. It was not that he was choosing suffering — he was choosing love. The choice cost him dear. In the garden of Gethsemane he cried out in human agony as he realised where his choice was leading him. But he went on to let his life be taken away to convince you and me that love is all that really matters and that love is stronger than death. So he dies for us, for you and me, that we might hear the message and take it seriously. He tells us that he believes we are worth dying for. If I see his death as a love story, then it can release a spring of love within me which will be a source of great new power to love as he loved.

16

SUFFERING IS NOT SENT

Jesus who is God dies for his people. He dies the most shameful death of a slave. Surely Jesus has turned upside down all our ideas about God? What kind of God is this? A God who dies out of love for weak people? This is not the idea most people have when they say the word 'God'. They think of God as infinitely powerful and wise. No wonder people rejected Jesus. But the first witnesses remained true to the God revealed by Jesus.

> While the Jews demand miracles and the Greeks look for wisdom, here are we preaching a crucified Christ; to the Jews an obstacle that they cannot get over, to the pagans madness, but to those who have been called, whether they are Jews or Greeks, a Christ who is the power and the wisdom of God. For God's foolishness is wiser than human wisdom, and God's weakness is stronger than human strength.
>
> (1 Co 1:22-25)

Paul could not have dared to say these things unless they had been revealed. For a Jew it would be a terrible blasphemy to speak of foolishness or weakness in God. But Jesus is God made visible, as Paul himself says, 'the love of God made visible' (Rm 8:39). Calvary tells us that another name for God is compassion. The word compassion means 'to suffer with someone'.

Surely it is true to say that Calvary is the 'wisdom' of God. What is one of the greatest problems that troubles the human heart? Is it not the terrible problem of evil and the suffering it brings, especially the suffering of innocent people? One of the greatest temptations against faith, against the existence of God, is the suffering in our world. Again and again we complain to God, 'Why do you allow such suffering? If you are real and have all power, why do you not prevent suffering?' We cannot, as it were, 'solve' this problem. We cannot explain it away with a formula of words. But if we are to cope in any way with the problem of suffering, we must return to Calvary and the mystery of God in Jesus dying on the cross. We might say that this was Jesus' way of dealing with the problem of suffering. Jesus did not argue about suffering. He did not ask the Father, 'Why do you allow suffering?' He did not see it as something to be understood; he saw it as something to be overcome by love. It was his love for his people that brought him to the cross. We have a God who is no stranger to suffering. He is not sitting out there on a cloud, indifferent to our pain. In some way he is present and even enduring the suffering with you and me. On the road to Damascus, Paul heard the cry, 'Saul, Saul, why are you persecuting me?' 'Who are you, Lord?', he asked, and the voice answered, 'I am Jesus, and you are persecuting me' (Ac 9:4-6).

Suffering is an evil and we must seek to prevent it, but when it comes, we must not let it conquer us. Endured with love, it is saved from becoming waste. Love can transform and overcome it. Such love is possible by the awareness that God is right there in the centre of it, not 'sending' it, not causing it, but helping us to endure and to carry it. If God is anywhere, he is in the heart of human suffering. When the early Christians, the friends of Jesus, were suffering persecution by Saul, then Jesus was suffering. 'I am Jesus and you are persecuting me' (Ac 9:5). A saintly, contemplative nun shared this insight with me. She said, 'I could not believe in a God who does not suffer.'

Calvary is a love story. The cross is the language of love which identifies with loved ones who are suffering. When we watch someone we love suffering, are we not very uncomfortable because we cannot take their pain away from them into ourselves? We said that we should not see the cross of Jesus as punishment because it would give a false image of God the Father. It is important for another reason to avoid that way of thinking. It affects the way we look upon our own suffering and cross of life. If we see the cross of Jesus as punishment, there is a danger that we will see our own suffering or cross in life as punishment. You sometimes hear people saying 'This pain or suffering is a punishment from God for my sins', or, 'I think my son or daughter is now being punished by God for my sins.' Please do not say things like that. It is completely false. I know this is how we people think and act. We expect wrongdoing to be followed by punishment, but let us not attribute our way of thinking to God. One day when the disciples saw a blind man by the road side, they asked, 'Rabbi, who sinned, this man or his parents, for him to have been born blind?' 'Neither he nor his parents sinned', Jesus answered (Jn 9:2-3). And Jesus told them they would see God's power revealed through this man's blindness.

Do not think suffering is sent by God. Suffering is not 'sent' to us. It comes. Often it is the consequence of our sin and failure. Our actions have consequences. Sinful actions bring disorder and suffering. In the East there is a saying: 'If a man speaks or acts with an evil thought, pain follows him as surely as the wheel follows the foot of the ox that draws the carriage.' Even when the suffering comes through our own fault, through some moral weakness or failure, still, I believe, we should not see it as a punishment 'sent' by an angry God. God is God of love. True love suffers with the loved one and does everything possible to heal and to save. The father of the Prodigal Son was moved to pity by his son's condition, a condition that had been caused by the boy's own sins. When we suffer either as a result of our own sins or the sins of others, Jesus suffers with us, and his loving, caring presence will give us power to be patient and trusting. This kind of suffering will save us and others from the evil of sin. God will bring

good out of the evil. Let us trust this God despite everything, as Jesus himself did on the cross when all seemed
hopeless. 'My God, my God, why have you deserted me?'
(Mk 15:34). We can echo this cry. Can we then go on to say
with Jesus: 'Father into your hands I commit my Spirit' (Lk
23:46)? When suffering comes to us, let us try to bear it
with trust and love.

And when we see the sufferings of others, let us try to do
what we can to help the sufferer. In the words of the song,
'We are here to help each other, walk the mile and bear the
load.' We may not be able to do very much or contribute in
any heroic way but any expression of love, no matter how
small, has power beyond what we imagine.

Mother Teresa says: 'It is not what you do that matters,
but the love you put into what you do.' There is a line in a
song about her which says, 'She washes the feet of those
who will not walk tomorrow.' She pours out her love on
those who will be dead tomorrow. She does not see this as
a waste of effort. The dying person may be beyond the help
of medicine, but the heart of that person can still be healed
by love and that love in some mysterious way becomes
greater than the suffering. We quoted already the words of
the old man disfigured by dirt, disease and suffering who
was dying in her arms and said: 'How strange that I who
have lived like an animal should die like an angel.'

There is the story of the man who was reflecting on this
great problem of suffering. In his heart he was questioning
God and complaining. He said: 'Lord, you see so much suffering. What are you doing about it?' and the Lord's voice
came back, 'I created you.' We all have a responsibility to
do what we can to help others who are suffering. Each
Christian is empowered to love. We have been set free from
sin, fear, guilt, free for loving. Each of us has the power to
bring into our world more help, healing, joy and love.

17

A NEW CREATION IN CHRIST

The central truth of our Christian faith is that we are saved by the passion, death and resurrection of Jesus. We speak of these saving events as the Paschal mystery. Here we mean mystery not in the sense of something the mind cannot understand but something that fills the heart with wonder and praise which no words can properly express. The word 'paschal' comes from the scriptural word 'pasch' or 'passover'. The great revelation of God's love in the death and resurrection of Jesus took place in history at a time when the Jews were remembering and celebrating another great sign of God's love for the chosen people, their delivery from slavery in the land of Egypt. For the Jews this was the great proof that Yahweh not only existed but that he cared. God had entered into their history and through Moses led them out of slavery into freedom. Pharaoh did not give up his captive people easily. God worked great signs and struck down the first-born of Egypt. The angel of vengeance 'passed over' the houses of Jewish families because their doorposts were marked by the blood of a lamb that had been sacrificed on the orders of Moses. This was the Passover they were to remember and celebrate all through their history after they had reached the Promised Land.

It was this great religious festival of the Passover that Jesus and his twelve apostles were celebrating at the Last Supper. But Jesus was introducing a new Pasch by challenging not just the might of any Pharaoh but the might and power of sin and evil. The deep meaning of what Jesus was doing was not appreciated by his followers until after his death and resurrection. It was only then that they began to realise they were involved in a great mystery, a great revelation of God, of his love, his wisdom, his power, and that it was something meant not for Jews alone but for all peoples. This truth dawned slowly on Christ's followers, but when they began to realise what had happened, they were transformed. They became new people with new vision and power. The Spirit came upon the believers and they now knew Jesus was amongst them still. The Spirit was not taking the place of Jesus, but was making him present in a new way. Paul says: 'Even if we did once know Christ in the flesh, that is not how we know him now' (2 Co 5:16). But it was the same Jesus, yesterday, today, always. He was present in the breaking of bread, he was present when they prayed, he was present in the people they met and present in the heart of each one. The promise had come true, 'We will come to him and make our dwelling place with him' (Jn 14:23). This was the Kingdom Jesus had spoken about, God really present all the time and actively present, healing, liberating, re-creating. God was not confined to holy places or holy times but God, who is Spirit, is found everywhere. Jesus brought fullness of life as he had promised. Fear of sin and guilt were overcome, the spirit of the children of God took their place. God was Abba and they were family and showed their new love by caring and by sharing goods and possessions (Ac 2:45).

Earlier we asked what it meant to say that Jesus died for our sins. We reflected on this for some time because it is so important and also because it can be misunderstood and bring fear instead of love. But we must be careful not to exaggerate the sin aspect of our redemption as if the whole purpose of the Paschal mystery was to wash away personal sins. The salvation won for us was a far richer reality than the forgiving of individual sins. It is nothing less than a new life, a whole new way of living, thinking and acting. God promises in prophecy: 'Now I am making the whole creation new' (Rv 21:5). Jesus came and said: 'I have come so that they may have life and have it to the full' (Jn 10:10). Jesus did not come to patch us up, as it were, he came to re-create us. 'No one puts a piece of unshrunken cloth on to an old cloak' (Mt 9:16). To Nicodemus he expressed the idea dramatically, 'You have to be born again' (Jn 3:3). Paul, in the letter to the Ephesians, after praying for our hidden self to grow strong, says, we are destined to be 'filled with the utter fullness of God' (Ep 3:9), and elsewhere he says 'For anyone who is in Christ, there is a new creation' (2 Co 5:17).

The evil in the world, the evil within us which prevents us being what we should be has been overcome. Christ our champion and our elder brother challenged those forces of evil. Calvary was the climax of that battle. There it seemed that Christ had lost and his followers were in complete disarray. All their hopes were dashed and their dreams shattered.

But then strange things began to happen. Different followers met him in different places and situations, on the public road, in the garden, at a meal, down by the lakeside, on the way to Damascus. And they had no doubt. They really met him and he was the same Jesus, and yet, in some ways, different with new powers. But it was him. They would lay their lives on the line for that and very many did. And when they found him again, they also found each other in a new and beautiful way. This was so obvious that unbelievers could not help noticing. They used to say, 'See how these Christians love one another.'

Yes, our sins are forgiven by the Paschal mystery, but so much more. It is the very root of sin that is destroyed by the victory of Jesus. He claimed that he came as a physician, a healer. A good doctor is not satisfied just to remove pain by giving out pain-killers. He tries to get to the root of the illness and heal there. Jesus came to attack the root of all sin — fear, guilt, selfishness. He attacks these things by revealing the true face of God, a face of love and compassion. The brightness and beauty of God's glance can burn out dark fear and guilt. This God in turn reveals to me my true hidden self and invites me to believe in that deep goodness within me. He is a God who says, 'I considered you worth dying for. Accept yourself and your gifts as I accept you. Stop wasting time in guilt and fear. Use this time for loving. Accept each other as I accept you, and share what I have given you. I set you free from sin, not that you might have a safe, cosy, selfish life, but that you might be able to turn to others with conviction that love is possible. Selfishness can be overcome. You can help me to make all creation new.'

18

MEETING THE RISEN LORD

The Paschal mystery is not a past event. It happens now. It is the good news for today. In his first homily Jesus described his message as 'good news' or gospel (Lk 4:18). It is Jesus himself, not St Luke, who chooses the expression 'good news'. He did not say he had come to give 'good advice'. If he had said that, it would mean he had come to tell people what they had to do. No! The message is 'news', which means something that is happening, not something I am doing but something others are doing. Here the news is what God is doing or wants to do among his people, healing, liberating them. So Jesus in his homily does not tell the congregation what they have to do to please God. They are already pleasing to God. Jesus tells them instead what God wants to do for them.

It is 'news' also because it is happening right now. When you buy your newspaper you expect to read 'news', to read of events happening now around you. You don't expect to read history. So the Paschal mystery is news. It is happening now. As Jesus said at the end of his homily, 'This text is being fulfilled now as you listen' (Lk 4:22). In his homily Jesus used a famous text from Isaiah describing the wonderful works of God which would happen in the days of the Messiah. The Jews were familiar with this text in their worship and liturgy. Up to that moment when Jesus read it, it was only a prophecy, looking to the future. But now with the presence of Jesus it is fact and reality — it is news. Unfortunately, when we read it today it is still as prophecy, as if the Kingdom was not among us. Or, maybe worse, we read it as history, the great things that happened in those far-off early years of the Church.

We must not see Jesus as if he were standing at some

mid-point in history with certain things happening before him and after him. No! Jesus stands at the end-point of history. These are the latter days in which you and I live. I do not mean that the end of the world is about to happen, but, much more important, the Kingdom has happened, it is among us. Jesus is risen and present and among us with the victory over evil and sin and offering us the power of that victory. He is risen and present and you and I can meet him and know him personally and be transformed by him as the early followers were.

Let us look at a meeting between the Risen Jesus and two of his first followers (Lk 24:13-35). Two of the disciples of Jesus are so discouraged and disillusioned by the events of Friday that they decide to get away from it all. They leave Jerusalem, the city of shattered dreams, and set out for a village called Emmaus. On the road they are joined by a 'stranger' who notices how upset they are and asks them why they are so sad. They tell him about their master and the tragedy of Calvary and he begins to console them.

What a revelation this is of the kindness and gentleness of Jesus and of his deep understanding. He has suffered so much, being rejected by his own people, tortured by foreigners and abandoned by his closest friends and followers. Despite all this he now spends time with two of those followers, cheering them up and renewing their hope. Note that there is no judging, no scolding, no bullying. He does not complain as we would, 'Where were you last Friday?' His whole concern is for them. He still loves them and wants to restore their faith and joy. He accepts them as they are and gives them what they need. He opens their eyes so that they can understand what has happened in Jerusalem. He shows them that it was not a series of chance happenings. God was still in control all the time. God was working out his plan of salvation despite all the evil people were capable of. The resurrection was not merely the reversal of evil or the turning of the tables on his enemies. The resurrection was fulfilment and it was for all of us. 'He not only died for us but rose for us' (Rm 8:34).

The two men listen and later tell us that their hearts began to burn within them as their hope and joy was renewed. When they reach Emmaus they press the stranger to join them for a meal. They ask him to share out the bread and as he does so they recognise Jesus. But then suddenly he was gone, vanished. And now we see the two men changed, full of life and enthusiasm, eager to get back quickly and tell the others what had happened on the way. They had wanted to get far away from Jerusalem. Now with a new flame in their hearts they cannot get back quickly enough.

I am certain that all followers of Jesus should expect to have some experience similar to that of these two ordinary disciples of Jesus. Somewhere, sometime, on the road of life, Jesus will join us and walk with us. And he will not be immediately recognisable as the Lord.

It may often be in a time of disappointment or disillusionment, as with these two on the way to Emmaus. It may be at a time when hopes have faded, dreams have been shattered and life has lost meaning — a bereavement, a sickness, a failure, a broken romance. We feel we want to get away from it all. It's too much for us and we cannot cope. Jesus often joins us then and introduces himself by asking 'Why are you so sad? What has happened that you are so low?' Tell him, simply and honestly, and you will find that he will speak and say that he knows and understands. Then he will show you the reality hiding under the events. They are not mere chance. God was there with you, loving you and bringing good out of the evil. He can now heal you and restore hope. He will help you to return to daily activity, to the place of broken dreams, with new power because you know he is in your heart. You are not alone and God is in control.

Or God will often join us on the road of life in some joyful event. It is often at a time of human celebration when we are experiencing real, unselfish joy that we experience something much greater than ourselves which we cannot describe or name. It may be when we fall in love, or celebrate the birth of a baby, or shed a tear at a wedding, or receive a visit from a very dear friend from the past. We feel there is something here that is very good and true, something that was meant to last, something that echoes in the deepest part of our self, something greater than our self. This again is a sign of God, of Jesus present, explaining life, opening the scripture of life to reveal the deeper meaning, assuring us that we are right to feel that joy should last for we are made for joy. Sorrow will be turned into joy. 'I will change their mourning into gladness' (Jr 31:13). God's final word is always joy, life, love, celebration.

Some meet Jesus in silent prayer alone or at a prayer meeting with others. Jesus loves to join in when two or three gather in his name. Some experience him in scripture, in a song or a religious ceremony. They feel that in some way they recognise the Lord. They have the experience of the Emmaus disciples. Jesus is not dead after all. He is risen, he is alive, he is near and really cares and walks and talks with us.

The heart of our religion is a living, loving, personal relationship with the Risen Lord. If our hidden self is to grow we must meet and experience the Lord in a personal way. We must pass over from an assent of the mind to an assent of the heart, from knowing about Jesus to knowing Jesus. All Christians know about Jesus the Lord but many do not know him as a personal friend. There is such a difference between 'knowing about' a person or place and 'knowing' the person or place.

It is the wish of Jesus that we should know him personally as a friend. He will come to us but often in disguise. The first followers who had lived with him for three years did not recognise him immediately when he met them after the Resurrection. One reason was simply that they did not expect to meet him. They were sure he was dead.

That might also be part of our problem. Maybe we see Jesus as a figure of history to be met in the pages of the gospel, having as much reality as a character from one of his own parables.

But Jesus is real and very much alive and seeking our friendship. One place to meet him is in private personal prayer. Indeed, if there were no such prayer in our lives it would be very difficult for friendship with Jesus to grow or for us to experience the joy of those early followers who discovered he was really alive. To know a friend we must spend time together. Sometimes when we read a certain scripture text, or hear a talk or listen to a hymn, we can feel a warmth and a love for Jesus. But if this is to grow and mature, time is needed. You know how we all rejoice when we see the first signs of spring. We rejoice because this is promise. Now there will be growth, food, fresh grass and flowers. But for this growth rain will be needed. The ground must be well soaked for real growth to come. In our Christian life it is good that we occasionally experience great joy in a word of scripture or a hymn or an inspiring sermon. But for real growth which will produce lasting fruit we need time in prayer so that our dry hearts may be soaked in God's love.

But many Christians will say, 'I'm too busy and can't find time for such prayer'. But if you don't spend time with God, how will the friendship grow? The cares of the world will crowd God out and little by little you will forget him. 'Out of sight, out of mind.' This proverb can apply to God as well as to men. If a man telephones his girlfriend to say, 'I'm sorry. I'm working late and can't make it this evening', there is nothing wrong. But if he makes this call a hundred times and does not see her for weeks, we have to doubt his love. A lover will overcome all difficulties to meet his beloved. The success and fruitfulness of a friendship cannot be left to one partner for too long.

19

WITNESSING TO THE GOOD NEWS

Have you ever noticed when you hear some very good news how eager you are to share it? At school, if you were the first to hear that, for some reason or other, the school term was ending earlier than expected and there would be an extra week's holiday, you would be 'bursting' to get back to your pals to tell them! If a baby is born in your family, it gives you great joy to tell your neighbours and friends. If a friend close to death makes a complete recovery, you want to share your joy with others. If you have discovered a beautiful new song, you will want to share it with your best friend.

Something very beautiful is happening here. Good and wonderful experiences move our hearts to share them and, when we do, our own joy increases in the sharing. When admiring wonderful natural scenery or enjoying good music, does it not mean even more to us when someone is with us, especially a close friend? What is happening here is not something merely natural and human. This is something divine in us and tells us we are more than we seem to be. It is one of those signs we spoke of which invite us to look at a deeper reality beneath the surface of daily life. This is how God is. He enjoys sharing goodness. And there is a bit of God in us. We are made in his likeness, that's why we enjoy sharing good news.

I am sure Jesus had this experience in a big way. He came from the Father with Good News and he was really eager to share it with us his friends. Before the Last Supper he said, 'I have longed to eat this Passover with you before I suffer' (Lk 22:15). Jesus was thrilled to tell us the good news of who we are and what his Father and our Father was really like, and how precious we are to that Father. One day he suddenly shouted out, 'I bless you Father, Lord of heaven and earth, for hiding these things from the learned and the clever and revealing them to mere children' (Mt 11:25). Jesus knew and loved the Father and took joy in revealing him and making him known.

If we get to know Jesus as a personal friend and discover how wonderful he is and fall in love with him and if we understand, even a little, the good news he brought to us, I think we too will want to tell others, to introduce others to Jesus and share with them the love he has given us. Earlier in this book we read the story of the meeting between Jesus and the woman at the well of Jacob. That woman was really thrilled at meeting Jesus. At the end of the story we read, 'The woman put down her water jar and hurried back to the town to tell the people' (Jn 4:29). Note, she had come to the well for water, but now she leaves it behind! It does not seem so important now compared with the spring of living water she has found in Jesus and his friendship. She is excited. She 'hurried back' to the town. Carrying the water jar would only slow her down. She leaves it behind.

We also spoke earlier of those two disappointed disciples meeting Jesus on the way to Emmaus. When they realised it was Jesus they were with, they forgot all about what they had wanted to do in Emmaus. When Jesus vanished from their sight, we are told that 'they set out that instant and returned to Jerusalem to tell their story of what had happened on the way' (Lk 24: 33-35). We know all this happened when the day was already far spent, but still they could not wait till next morning. 'They set out that instant.'

In the Acts of the Apostles, we read about the early Christians and the first days of the Church, the new Christian community. We find they are an excited people. Something fantastic had happened which changed their lives and they just had to talk about it. Jesus, their friend and leader, had overcome death and was now amongst them, never to leave them, and he had brought them power, hope, love. They rejoiced in it and talked about it and it led them to a new love for each other. Also it brought them an extraordinary new courage to bear persecution and hatred and even death. When they were flogged for speaking about Jesus and his resurrection, we are told,'They left the presence of the Sanhedrin glad to have had the honour of suffering humiliation for the sake of the name' (Ac 5:41).

What we are talking about here is Christian witnessing. This is what Jesus had spoken of before his ascension. 'You will be my witnesses' (Ac 1:8). We must not think of witnessing as some kind of Christian duty, an exercise I have to do if I am to be a good Christian. No, it is something utterly natural, sharing with others the joy and happiness he has brought us. Why do more Christians not witness this way? Maybe the reason is that they have not met Jesus in this way, may not yet have experienced his healing and his power in their lives. The early Christians were excited because something fantastic had happened and they had to talk about it. Many Christians today are not excited people! Why? Maybe, in a sense, they do not feel that anything fantastic has happened. But it has! Jesus is risen and is amongst us and we can meet him in prayer, in scripture, in sacrament and in serving each other.

A Christian witness is one who by his very life is saying, 'Jesus Christ is alive and with us and we can put all our trust in him.' He is not claiming to be morally perfect. He is not setting himself up as a model of perfection, someone who has all the answers and keeps all the rules and is always denouncing sin and human weakness. This is not witnessing. Indeed it is the opposite and will turn people away from God. The witness by his or her life lives in the truth that God is their Father, that this Father is compassion and healing and will save them from eternal death, that the Risen Jesus is their brother and the power of the Spirit is given to know Jesus and grow like him.

With St Paul we say that we are not perfect but we keep trying. Witnessing will mean showing patience in times of adversity, forgiving those who offend us, showing concern for those suffering from sickness, bereavement, poverty, injustice, loneliness, showing tolerance and charity towards those who differ from us in beliefs, having compassion for human weakness and defending the values of Christ. This was the way of our Lord. We must try to be like him. In as much as we succeed with his help we are making him present in our time. The world needs such witnesses because it needs him so much.

Unbelievers in the world today cry out for true, credible witnesses. They are tired of religious arguments and discussions and hypocrisy. They say to us, 'We don't want your arguments and discourses. Just show us what it would be like if we did believe and commit ourselves.' They are not asking us to be saints, free from every tiny moral fault. They want to know if love, hope, unselfishness and joy are possible in this world. In the prophet Zechariah we are told what people are looking for. 'In those days ten men of nations of every language will take a Jew by the sleeve and say, "We want to go with you since we have learnt that God is with you."' (Zach 8:20). Notice what attracts them to the Jew. Why do they want to go with him? Because they have seen that God is with him. People want to see some evidence in our times that God is with us. People are quick to spot a phoney religious person —one who 'prays' and keeps the rules but has not the love and compassion of Jesus. The scribes and Pharisees should have been witnesses but instead they turned people away from God.

We should not be surprised then at the power Jesus exercised over the people. They could see that God was with him. They could see how different he was from the scribes. 'His teaching made a deep impression on them, because, unlike the scribes, he taught them with authority' (Mk 1:22). Jesus was witnessing to the Father's love and compassion. He was the greatest witness. By his words and deeds he was simply and powerfully saying, 'This is what your Father is like.' St Paul describes Jesus as 'the love of God made visible' (Rm 8:39).

Finally, we can say that if a Christian does not in some way witness to Christ, does not share his faith, then that faith could become a private affair and would not be what Jesus brought and witnessed to. Jesus once described his mission this way. 'I have come to bring fire to the earth, and how I wish it were blazing already' (Lk 12:49). It is an interesting image. Fire needs to set alight whatever it touches, otherwise it dies. If a fire runs into a river or a wall, it dies. Fire remains alive as long as it is communicating itself. Faith is something like that.

20

THE GREATEST IS LOVE

St Paul, writing to the Corinthians about the different gifts of the Holy Spirit, encourages them to desire the greatest of the gifts which is love. There can be no true authentic witnessing to Christ without love. Indeed, all other forms of witnessing, says Paul, would be empty without love. Eloquent preaching, prophecy, almsgiving, even martyrdom would be useless unless inspired by love. This is a sobering thought for us all. St John of the Cross says, 'At the sunset of life we will all be judged on love.'

Mother Teresa of Calcutta tells how she was once in Europe collecting for her work in India when she got news of heavy storms and flooding in a district in India where she was working. Many poor people were left homeless. She was greatly disturbed at the news and spoke to a certain priest, sharing with him her distress and near-despair. She said to the priest, 'Father, how can I go back to those poor people and talk to them about the love of God?' The priest gave her a profound answer. He said, 'Mother, go back to those people. But don't talk to them about the love of God, be the love of God to them.' This was how Jesus witnessed. He made God's love visible. We are called to be other Christs.

The most authentic form of witnessing is loving service to our brethren in their different needs. There are so many in need of our loving help — the sick, the hungry, the oppressed, the AIDS patient, the lonely, the bereaved, the exploited. Jesus gives a list in the parable of the final judgment (Mt 15: 31-46). We must approach those suffering people with great reverence. We must be certain in our hearts that they are precious to God and loved by him as they are right now. We must have no doubts about God's unconditional love for them. If we have, then we will not be a channel for God's healing power and love to them. We are supposed to be letting God's love flow to them, not blocking it. Jesus was able to heal and touch hidden springs of growth and love because he knew these broken people were the beloved of his Father and his own heart went out in love to them. He conveyed this in the way he related to them.

We have to try and love like this.'Love one another, as I have loved you' (Jn 15:12). This means we too must accept people as we find them. We also must try to give our love without condition. We must not wait for people to change, to 'improve', to reach some standard we have set for them before we love them. Our work is not to change people but to love them. To accept people as they are does not mean we want them to stay as they are. We naturally want everyone to grow and find more meaning in life. Growth always involves some change in life for us all. But the condition for growth is accepting love. Paul prayed for us all to be planted in God's love so that we might grow in Christ (Ep 3:17).

When Jesus was asked which was the most important commandment, he answered, 'You must love the Lord your God with all your heart, with all your soul, with all your mind and with all your strength' (Mk 12:30). I used to have a problem with this commandment. If I give my whole heart to God, what is left for my neighbour? I was helped by a certain preacher. He said we must not think of love as a kind of substance to be cut up and shared out like a cake. Love is not divisible in that way. He gave this example. A little girl loves her Dad with her whole heart. Then she grows up, falls in love, marries and loves her husband with her whole heart. Does she now love her Dad less? No, surely not! Then she has a baby whom she loves with her whole heart. Does that mean she takes something away from her husband? Again, no! There is no competition between these loves. So with our love for God and for

97

our neighbour. These loves are not competing. Indeed, the opposite is true, these loves nourish each other. If I really love God, I will certainly love his children, my neighbours. And the more genuinely my heart goes out to people in unselfish love, the more I will be drawn to God.

Here is a story which was made into a film entitled *The Fourth Wise Man*.

A certain good and kind man lived at the time Jesus was born. He hears about the three wise men who came to the land of the Jews searching for a new King who had been born. He too wants to find this King and worship him. He sells his property, buys gifts for the new King and sets out in search. He arrives too late to find the three wise men who have gone back on a different road to their own country. He continues searching in different places for many years. He is a compassionate man and keeps getting side-tracked by people with different needs, poor people, sick people, lepers, prisoners. Over the years he gives away nearly all his gifts to help these people. Then he hears of strange events in a place called Judaea. Someone claiming to be King of the Jews is in trouble with the authorities. He continues his journey and arrives in Jerusalem. But he is late again, the 'King' has been condemned and has been taken to the place of execution. The man, now old and tired, hurries towards Calvary. On the way he meets a detachment of Roman soldiers leading a Jewish girl to slavery. The girl breaks away from the soldiers and runs to him and begs him to ransom her, to buy her freedom. By now he has only one gift left for the King, a precious pearl. It could buy the girl's freedom. He hesitates, but finally gives her the precious stone. She is saved. Then he hurries on to the hill of Calvary but when he arrives, the crosses are empty. All is over, he is late again.

Now, tired and weary, he sets out for home but on the way becomes ill. He finds a quiet spot beside the road and lies down to rest and die. As he rests, a shadow falls across him. He looks up at the person standing over him. In the film we do not see the Lord, only the shadow. The dying man's face lights up with wonder and joy. The one looking down on him is wearing a crown. The old man says, 'I have been searching for you all the years but now it is you who has found me.' But then a look of great disappointment crosses the old man's face. 'And on the day I meet you, I have nothing left to give you. All has been given away.' The Lord speaks: 'Do not be disappointed. For you gave all these gifts to me, when you gave them to others in need. And now arise and let us finish this journey together.'

This story is based on the famous parable about the final judgment (Mt 25: 31-46). Those who enter the kingdom are those who give loving service to the suffering. Notice that Jesus' list of sufferers includes prisoners, who are often responsible for their own suffering. This does not matter to Jesus. He identifies with them. In this parable it is very important to notice that those whom the Lord welcomes into his Kingdom are very surprised. They had not realised that they were helping Christ when they were loving people. This is a deep point. Sometimes we meet self-righteous people who practise a kind of 'cold' charity. They almost use others to win a reward for themselves. But this would be the opposite of what Jesus wants to teach here. Jesus wants people to get the focus off themselves on to those who are suffering. He is not trying to motivate people to go out and practise charity so they can please God in heaven and save their own souls. This would simply encourage a kind of spiritual selfishness.

In this parable Jesus is making a deep statement about a basic reality which is that God identified with suffering people and if I help anyone with love, then God is there and I am helping him.

Again, there is no competition in the loving. I love people, not indirectly for God's sake, but directly with God's love which has been given to me precisely for this purpose. "The love of God has been poured into our hearts by the Holy Spirit which has been given to us" (Rm 5:5). This, the greatest of the gifts, has been given generously to us so that we may share it. Loving our neighbour is not a precondition for the coming of God's Kingdom on earth, it is a sign that the Kingdom is among us. Jesus came to set us free from fear, guilt and preoccupation with sin, but, more importantly, to free us for loving. When the early Christians realised this, that Jesus was alive and among them and accepting them and not scolding them for the past, then they turned to each other in new love and sharing. They became conscious of their unity in faith and love as the body of Christ. If one was in need, the whole body suffered and was concerned. Their power to overcome their human selfishness came from their joyful acceptance of the love of God poured into their hearts by the Holy Spirit.

'Love one another as I have loved you' (Jn 15:12). This is the high ideal put before us Christians. We will never rise to this ideal unless we accept the unconditional love he offers us. There and there only is the source of our power to love one another as Christ asks. This is why we should humbly and joyfully accept his love. It is given to me not for myself alone, but for others. It is like all God's gifts. It is meant to be shared with others. Most of the time I will not have the opportunity to do anything great or heroic in the way of charity, but each of us will find chances to do something, no matter how small. Mother Teresa says: 'It is not what you do that matters but the love you put into what you are doing.' Any kind word or deed, even if at the time it goes unnoticed or unappreciated, will always bear fruit.

'I was sick and you visited me' (Mt 25:36). These words

of Christ will present a special new challenge to many
Christians in our day because of the terrible new sickness
of AIDS in our world. AIDS is spreading with such terrify-
ing speed that soon there will be few families untouched by
the disease through either the illness or death of a relative
or friend. Many Christians will be challenged to become
personally involved in helping people with AIDS. Because
AIDS is spread by sexual contact it is a sensitive matter and
some may feel shame which could lead them to hide their
problem. We must help them to overcome this shame by
showing Christ's loving compassion with no trace of judgment. Those who suffer from AIDS say one of the hardest
things to bear is the sense of loneliness. Some people out of
ignorance keep away from them, fearing infection. We
should all know there is absolutely no risk of infection from
ordinary social contact like shaking hands, hugging, sharing food from the same dish or using the same utensils.
Medically we are not able to cure AIDS but we can help the
patient greatly by loving acceptance and ordinary daily
friendship. There is a cure for the painful and destructive
emotions that rise in the heart of an AIDS patient, the
shame, fear, loneliness, anger. There is one person who can
calm this storm and that is Jesus. We must introduce the
patient to Jesus and his love, to Jesus who turns everything
to our good, even our sins, failure and sickness. We know
that AIDS patients are mostly young and they feel how
hard it is to die young before their dreams are realised.
Jesus can help them by opening their eyes to a wider vision
of life. He can show them that the value of their lives is not
measured by achievements, success, length of years. It is
measured by loving union with God, by accepting the salvation offered freely by God now, no matter what kind of
life they have led up to this point. The AIDS crisis need not
be the end of everything. Indeed, it can be the beginning of
something new and beautiful. A true witness will help
AIDS sufferers to see this.

We all move along the road of life together. Jesus walks

with us as he did with the two disciples going to Emmaus. Witnessing means helping each other to recognise Jesus with us on the way. In our song we say:

> Brother, let me be your servant
> Let me be as Christ to you.
> We are pilgrims on a journey
> We are brothers on the road.
> We are here to help each other
> Walk the mile and bear the load.

On life's journey we must be ready to carry each other when the load of sorrow, problems and sickness becomes too heavy. But we shall not be able to do this, unless we are convinced that we ourselves are carried by God.

21

GOD CARRIES HIS PEOPLE

We will not be able to carry each other, unless we are sure that we ourselves are carried by God. Listen to a beautiful word from God which assures us that this in fact is the reality. God does carry his people through life.

> And I said to you: Do not take fright, do not be afraid of your enemies. Yahweh your God goes in front of you and will be fighting on your side as you saw him fight for you in Egypt. In the wilderness too, you saw him: how Yahweh carried you, as a man carries his child, all along the road you travelled on the way to this place. But for all this, you put no faith in Yahweh your God who had gone in front of you on the journey to find you a camping ground, by night in the fire to light your path, by day in the cloud (Dt 1:29-33) .

Moses is speaking to the people, encouraging them to trust in God by reminding them how God had delivered them from Egypt. He reminds them of that deeper reality which gives meaning to their lives, the presence of a loving active God who cares for them, not because they are great or famous as a nation but just because he has set his heart on them (Dt 7:7-8).

Let us concentrate on one verse from this passage: 'Yahweh has carried you, as a man carries his child, all along the road you travelled on the way to this place.' (v31). Notice the image God uses in this inspired word. God carries us as a father lifts his child up into his arms or on to his shoulder to carry him when he is tired. Think about this. God carries his people. God carries you and me. Do you believe this? Do you experience this? For some people it seems to be almost the other way round.

The prophet Isaiah, in several places, mocks the false gods of the pagans which have 'eyes' that do not see and 'ears' which cannot hear and 'mouths' which do not speak. In one passage he describes how the woodcutter goes out into the forest and cuts down a tree. He keeps the larger branches for firewood and for cooking. Then he takes the trunk and shapes it into an image, carving eyes, ears, mouth. He brings this god to his hut and worships. What happens when his village is attacked by an enemy? This man runs into the hut, lifts out his god on to a donkey and carries the god to safety (Is 44:9-20; 46:1-2). But, says Isaiah, it is not so with our God, the true God. He is the one who carries us to safety.

> You have been carried since birth, whom I have carried since the time you were born. In your old age I shall be still the same, when your hair is grey I shall still support you. I have already done so, I have carried you, I shall still support and deliver you (Is 46:3-4).

God reveals himself as the God who carries. But many Christians do not seem to experience God in this way. Unfortunately, many seem to experience God as a burden which they have to carry. What do I mean by this? Well, God for many is distant, 'up there' somewhere, watching them to make sure they keep the commandments. Such a God inspires fear. Religious duties are observed and commandments kept to please and win his favour. This kind of religion is more like magic where we try to control God by certain ceremonies and words. And it becomes a religion of fear because we know our weakness and how often we fail to keep commandments, and so now there is fear of

punishment. Fear and guilt are added to all the other burdens of life we already carry. It should be the other way
round. The knowledge of God and his living presence
within us should be a source of power and strength to
carry these other burdens. Ask yourself: Does God carry
you or do you try to carry God? Does religion carry you or
do you feel you have to carry religion as a burden? If you
have met the true God, you are blessed. He is the God who
says: 'I have carried you since the time you were born. In
your old age I shall still be the same. I shall still support
and deliver you' (Is 46:4).

But if God loves and carries me, what about suffering in
my life? We said before that our experience of suffering
often leads us to doubt and question God: 'Why did you
allow this to happen? Where were you when this trouble
came?' The following passage from an unknown author
offers a reflection on this question:

One night I had a dream
I dreamed I was walking along the beach with
the Lord
Across the sky flashed scenes from my life
For each scene I noticed
two sets of footprints in the sand
One belonged to me and the other to the Lord
When the last scene of my life flashed before
me I looked back at the footprints in the sand
I noticed that many times along the path of my
life there was only one set of footprints
I also noticed that it happened at the very
lowest and saddest times in my life
This really bothered me
and I questioned the Lord about it;
'Lord, you said that once I decided to follow
you you would walk with me all the way
But I have noticed
that during the most troublesome times in my

life there is only one set of footprints
I don't understand why in times when
I needed you most, you should leave me.
The Lord replied,
My precious, precious child
I love you and I would never, never leave you
during your times of trial and suffering
When you saw only one set of footprints
It was then that I carried you.

Yes, God does carry us when life gets rough and we have heavy problems. And even if some of the problems are of our own making, this does not matter to God. Jesus described himself as the Good Shepherd who loves each single sheep as if it was the only one. If one foolish sheep were to stray away and get lost he would go searching for it in the wilderness.

And when he found it, would he not joyfully take it on his shoulders, and then, when he got home call together his friends and neighbours? Rejoice with me, he would say, I have found my sheep that was lost (Lk 15:5-6).

Here again is the same image, God carrying the lost sheep on his shoulders. And he carries it, not blaming it, but just rejoicing. Can anyone measure the love of such a God? As we are joyfully carried by God, let us in turn joyfully carry each other.

22

LIFE IS A STORY

We began this book by saying that the life of each one of us is a story, a story that has purpose, direction and deep meaning. I return to this thought now as we finish the book. Let us listen again to the Lord's word.

> Yahweh has carried you, as a man carries his child, all along the road you travelled on the way to this place (Dt 1:31).

Some years ago these words suddenly became alive and full of meaning for me, as if they were being spoken directly to me. They brought a great new blessing into my life, a blessing of peace and joy which I share with you now.

At that time I had been looking back on my life as a Christian and a priest and I felt discouraged by what I saw. I did not seem to have done anything worthwhile. My life did not have any special meaning. God seemed distant and impersonal. As a boy I believed in him mostly out of conformity. In the seminary I studied as best I could to know about God, the Bible, religion and the Church so that I could explain to others, answer their difficulties and encourage their faith. Often I was so busy working for God that I failed to find time for quiet personal prayer. Sometimes, I confess, I was glad to be busy because nothing ever happened in the prayer time and I thought I could do more working for God than 'wasting' time in apparently useless prayer. My life was drifting. I looked back on those years of ordinary work, much lukewarm service of God, plenty of immaturity, fears and selfishness. The years seemed wasted.

Then I was blessed in meeting a number of people who where involved in a renewal movement in the Catholic Church in the 1970s. They were lay people, nuns, brothers and priests. This was like a new beginning for me. Jesus became real and personal. The scriptures spoke in a living, direct way to me. There was a desire for personal prayer. God became for me the God who carries his people and the Father of the prodigal son. All this was possible because of God's Spirit given to me by Jesus and the Father. This Spirit was with me since Baptism, but somehow I had not realised the power that had been there all the time. I saw that my sins and failures were really forgiven and totally forgotten. Now instead of being a source of guilt, they were a cause for new joy because they only emphasised how wonderful God was and how patient. He had continued loving me so faithfully all through those years when I showed so little appreciation of his love. I knew I was among the late workers brought into the vineyard by the Lord and was receiving all this love not because I had earned it, but just because God was so good.

Then came a new temptation. I began to regret the past as wasted and wished that I had had these new insights when I was much younger. It was just then that I found those words from Deuteronomy and that this particular verse spoke so strongly to me, 'Yahweh has carried you all along the road you travelled on the way to this place.' Reading this verse I was able to see my whole life differently. This is the blessing I share with you.

In the light of this verse, I could look back and believe that my life is a story. My life is not a series of events, one just following another. It is a unified story. It is not a series of chance happenings. Every part of it is in God's loving hands. Nothing is wasted. Even the sins, failures and immaturity were all in God's hands. There is no need to throw away any part of it. There is no need for regret. Every bit of it was and is in God's care and he has touched and healed all the mean, ugly, sinful parts. Everything is healed. Everything is redeemed. Nothing is wasted, not even one tear. The healed scars of sin are evidence of his power and beauty. And what was true for my life up to that moment would be true for every moment to follow.

Life is a story and there are two authors, God and myself. God conceived me in his heart and wanted me to be. He loved me into life and wants me to grow and become like his son Jesus. But he also allows me my freedom. I must make my choices. I must co-write my story. Because of my weakness, I sin and fail but he continues to love me and recreate me and burn my sins away in the fire of his love. He never stops loving even when I become so unlike Jesus. After the many blessings he has given me I still fail him in many ways, still become afraid, often forget the Holy Spirit, still conform to the values of the world about me. Yet despite all this brokenness, it is not the same as before. I know his love is greater than my heart. He is infinitely patient and gentle. I am weak, but my weakness keeps me close to him and more open to his power. I also hope my weakness may keep me open to my brethren.

If God can love me in such a way, I feel I can say to everyone that God's love is greater than they can imagine. Paul says it is 'beyond all knowledge'. He prays that we may be planted in that love so that our hidden self may grow strong so that Christ may live in our hearts. We do not have to make a journey away from where we are or who we are to find Christ. He is in our hearts. He is the treasure hidden in the field of our hearts, the treasure that can transform our lives. He can open our eyes to see our life as a story in his hands, a story full of deep meaning, a story that, with his help, will have a happy ending. Let us finish with a prayer for all of us. It is Paul's prayer for his fellow Christians in Ephesus and I'm sure his prayer for us also:

This, then, is what I pray, kneeling before the Father, from whom every family, whether spiritual or natural, takes its name: Out of his infinite goodness, may he give you the power through his Spirit for your hidden self to grow strong, so that Christ may live in your hearts through faith, and then, planted in love and built on love, you will with all the saints have strength to grasp the breadth and the length, the height and the depth; until, knowing the love of Christ, which is beyond all knowledge, you are filled with the utter fullness of God.

Glory be to him whose power, working in us, can do infinitely more than we can ask or imagine; glory to him from generation to generation in the Church and in Christ Jesus for ever and ever. Amen (Ep 3:14-21).